Reclaiming Our Cities and Towns

RECLAIMING OUR CITIES AND TOWNS

Better Living with Less Traffic

David Engwicht

New Society Publishers
Philadelphia, PA Gabriola Island, BC

 Published in cooperation with envirobook, Australia

Inquiries regarding requests to reprint all or part of *Reclaiming Our Cities and Towns: Better Living with Less Traffic* should be addressed to:
New Society Publishers
4527 Springfield Avenue
Philadelphia, PA 19143

ISBN Hardcover   USA 0-86571-282-4   CAN 1-55092-226-2
ISBN Paperback   USA 0-86571-283-2   CAN 1-55092-227-0

Line drawings by Michael Gunn.
Cover design by Laura Joyce Shaw.
Cover photo by P.F. Bentley / Time Magazine.
Designed and typeset in 10/12 Garamond by Envirobook, Sydney NSW.

Printed on partially-recycled paper using soy ink by Capital City Press, Montpelier, Vermont.

To order directly from the publisher, add $2.50 to the price for the first copy, 75¢ each additional. Send check or money order to:

In the United States:	*In Canada:*
New Society Publishers	New Society Publishers
4527 Springfield Avenue	PO Box 189
Philadelphia, PA 19143	Gabriola Island, BC VOR 1XO

New Society Publishers is a project of the New Society Educational Foundation, a nonprofit, tax-exempt, public foundation in the United States, and of the Catalyst Education Society, a nonprofit society in Canada. Opinions expressed in this book do not necessarily represent positions of the New Society Educational Foundation, nor the Catalyst Education Society.

745-C

For my children Luke, Jodi and Nathan.

You gave us life
  and in return
We conquered
  dissected
    mechanised
      fouled the nest.
Forgive us
  take control
    lead us home.

Foreword

Just think: 70 per cent of the surface area of the city of Los Angeles is in some way dedicated to the motor car. Freeways, garages, buildings for parking, parking lots, factories...70 per cent! And one job in six, in the USA, is linked to the car industry; it's about one in ten in Australia.

In Bangkok recently, where there is no public transport worth speaking of and where roads have been built over swelling streams, there was a traffic jam stretching for 50 kilometres. Also, recently in Lyon, the second city of France, the mayor likened the relationship between motorists and residents to the Hundred Years War. In Stockholm the head of Volvo declared that the time had come to ban private motoring from the inner city.

A survey just published in Britain shows that motorists no longer expect pleasure from their driving, however elaborate their vehicles. It's become a chore. This is how the *Times* of London commented in an editorial:

> Traffic merely increases the boredom and succeeds in turning ennui to fury. Commuting by car in all but the most rural of areas is unpleasant, matched only by commuting by train, bus or Tube. The logic of yesterday's survey is that, instead of exploring other modes of transport, drivers may start to ask themselves the wartime question: 'Is my journey really necessary?' For those with enlightened employers, the answer may be, 'No'. A telephone, home computer and fax machine may do just as well. ('Driven to Despair', *Times*, 3/9/91)

Without even invoking clear and obvious concerns about pollution and greenhouse, it is clear the situation in the world's cities, including those of Australia, is grim. Yes, technology will deliver clever and cleaner cars, traffic studies will permit sophisticated planning of roads and flow will be pushed to the limit. But, as Gertrude Stein might have said: 'A jam is a jam is a jam!'

There are alternatives. Exciting ones. And they will make life quieter, cleaner, safer, more fun and more human. It will not be achieved with the approach of a Luddite but with that of a very modern scientist. We have the maths, the number-crunching machines and the experience to put with our sensible everyday needs as people. Cities are for us, not for juggernauts, concrete wastelands or muck. This book shows how we can reclaim our cities for the purpose they were created: decent living.

ROBYN WILLIAMS.
Chairperson, Commission For the Future.

Contents

Acknowledgements

Thanks to the Queensland Main Roads Department who, by deciding to put a 'freeway' through my suburb, started me on the journey that led to this book. Little did the department know that the pain they were unwittingly inflicting on those who would be uprooted (especially the senior citizens) became the motivation that sustained me through three long years of community action, research and reflection.

Thanks to the people older than myself, like Pat Cochrane, who shared their knowledge and taught me lessons about place, neighbourhood friendships and real quality of life.

Thanks to my parents who instilled in me a sense of fair play and justice, along with a stubborn streak. Thanks to my children and wife who endured my obsession.

Thanks to Nathalie, the members of the CART committee, the Australia Council and the organisers of the International Pedestrian Conference for making my overseas study tour possible and to those, like Professor Monheim, who gave so freely of their time while I was their guest.

Thanks to the thousands of extraordinary 'ordinary' people who shared with me their wisdom and insight at public meetings, on street corners and in shopping centres, not only during the Route 20 campaign, but in cities all over Australia. This book is also their wisdom and their insight.

Thanks to the hundreds of planning professionals and engineers: some of whom sharpened my insights and ideas through fierce debate; others who courageously provided me with invaluable forums for my ideas in seminars, universities and conferences; others who even more courageously invited me to participate as a partner in the planning process; and to those who became my friends and gave me invaluable advice.

Thanks to Michael Gunn for going beyond duty in the preparation of drawings and figures, to Jeff Kenworthy and Dr. Fred Bell for doing likewise with their detailed technical critiques.

Finally, thanks to Patrick Thompson, Rod Ritchie and Jennifer Gormley for their invaluable help in editing and preparing this manuscript for publication.

Introduction

Like most people, I once believed that building bigger and better roads was just part of progress. Where would our modern society be without the car? Of course I had never been forced to think the issue through. That was until September 1987 when a brochure arrived in my letter-box announcing a public meeting to discuss the 'upgrading' of Route 20, a road through our suburb in Brisbane, Australia. Although we lived two blocks from the actual route, our street was marked on the map as potentially affected by diverted traffic. My wife, Beverley, insisted we go – something she has doubted the wisdom of ever since!

At first I thought the whole project sounded like a reasonable idea – until a couple of residents explained that the project was part of an inner-western bypass for Brisbane. They talked about the de facto freeway's effect on our suburb. Someone else explained how bigger roads are not the solution to our transport needs in the city and only lead to worse traffic problems. What they said made a lot of sense. I became convinced the project should be opposed, so in my usual brash way, proposed that a community action group be established to fight the proposal. I walked out of the meeting as a member of a group which became known as CART, Citizens Against Route 20.

CART made a decision at its very first meeting which in retrospect was of monumental importance. We decided not to push the problem into some one else's backyard. As a result CART was forced to look for long term solutions to the problems of traffic in our cities.

About six months into our campaign we had won a freeze on the project while a social and environmental impact study was carried out. At the first meeting with the consultants they outlined how their computer modelling predicted a 57 per cent increase in traffic on Route 20. Something had to be done. One of the residents responded by detailing how the build up of traffic over the past fifteen years had eroded his family's quality of life; everything from being woken up at four in the morning by heavy trucks, to being forced to drive his children to school for safety reasons. 'I don't care what your predictions for the next twenty years are,' he explained, 'I want you to give me back some of the quality of life I have lost over the past fifteen years.' The consultants replied that this was impossible and only a utopian dream. I blurted out, 'Why?' That night I could not sleep. It was as if I had been handed a challenge. A mission.

The nature of CART's campaign took a new course. No longer were we fighting some *future* threat. We were dealing with a present problem.

The preoccupation became: is it possible to manage the movement of people and goods in a way that would result in more livable cities?

We spent days and weeks in libraries. We followed leads. Wrote letters to universities around the world. Telephoned. Even faxed Australian embassies in Denmark, Germany, Holland and Sweden. We discovered that a new planning ethos was emerging which was resulting in some cities adopting different policies. Some were taking road space back from cars and giving it over to pedestrians, cyclists and public transport. They were discouraging car use but providing positive alternatives.

In February 1989, because the consultants were due to release their report, CART decided to try to steal the grounds of debate by releasing an alternative report – one week before the consultants released theirs. At first we were going to photocopy a few copies of Traffic Calming – The Solution to Route 20 and a New Vision for Brisbane[1] and have them nicely bound, but two things changed our mind. Firstly, some academics who read the manuscript urged us to make it more widely available. Secondly, we found it was cheaper to have them printed, providing we were prepared to gamble on selling 500 copies.

Traffic Calming successfully grabbed the high ground with the consultants delaying the release of their report for a couple of months while they rewrote it to include traffic calming as their sixth option. But we were not prepared for the response to Traffic Calming from outside Brisbane. Requests flooded in from councils, consultants and community action groups from all over Australia and even overseas.

Looking back at the success of Traffic Calming sometimes causes a mild shudder in my spine. It was the result of twelve months of concerted thinking by a group of people who had no previous experience in traffic or town planning. Our thinking was still developing and evolving. We rushed to print for political reasons, even while many of the ideas were still fermenting and formulating. Yet this unpretentious piece of literature was being quoted widely as the bible on traffic and transport.

In September 1989, I addressed the International Pedestrian Conference in Boulder, Colorado and at the same time visited 19 cities in the US, Europe and England. In 1990 I wrote the first draft of this book, tentatively titled *Human Rights & The Car*, with the emphasis being on how current transport planning was infringing on a range of very basic human rights. For a year the manuscript lay on the floor.

The catalyst to rewrite the book was a paper that I delivered at the 1991 International Transport Conference,[2] the culmination of some thinking I had done after my overseas trip. I asked myself two questions: 'For what reason does humanity create and maintain cities?' and 'What is the role of transport in cities?' I concluded that cities are an invention to *maximise exchange* (culture, goods, friendship, knowledge) and *minimise travel.* The role of transport is to help maximise exchange. Although the answers seemed obvious, their implications for transportation were profound. For example, I concluded that an auto-dominated transport system may destroy more exchange opportunities than it opens up. It became clear that this new way of viewing transport provided a significant breakthrough that placed a whole new complexion on the role of movement in cities.

I was advised by an engineering friend that I should not present the paper I had written – the audience could read that at their leisure – but that I should talk about the *processes* that had led to its development. So I decided that instead of telling the conference *what* I had thought, I would tell them *how* I had thought; the thinking processes that had led to the conclusions of my paper. It was then I realised that I was using different thought processes from the mainstream planning professionals and that using these new thought processes opened up a whole new view of our cities. And so I felt compelled once again to pound the keyboard.

Many readers will at some time during this book have questions about my presuppositions. Allow me to set the record straight on five.

Are you anti-car? No, our family does own one – but we walk, cycle or use public transport wherever possible. This book is against the *inappropriate* use of cars. More importantly, it promotes pro-active ideas for creating more livable cities in which all of us will have greater freedom of choice in transport and an increased quality of life.

Are you anti-planners and anti-engineers? No, some of my best friends are from these professions. Sure, I attack a way of looking at the world which, while delivering many benefits, is now threatening the future of our planet. But overriding that attack is a pro-active promotion of a new way of thinking which will result in cities becoming dynamic eco-systems that further the well-being of *all* its inhabitants.

Are you anti-travel? No, but I am against being forced into *unnecessary* travel which is exactly what car-dependent cities do. I am also against forms of travel which destroy community life and impoverish the city environment. Obviously my own travels have contributed greatly to the insights of this book.

Will your ideas not promote greater government control? On the contrary, I believe it is time for communities to take control of their own destinies and not allow the status-quo or vested interests to dictate their future. As communities become enlightened about what contributes to their long-term well-being, they often need to make new rules for the way they live corporately. This process is the very basis of democratic freedom. Being flexible enough to admit past mistakes and change patterns of living is a mark of maturity.

Are you trying to force people into community life? A city should be a place where we can both find solitude and enjoy the richness of a diverse cosmopolitan city. The tragedy of our modern day cities is that the choice to enjoy the latter has been removed for many people.

Reclaiming Our Cities and Towns is a record of my evolving understanding. Even as I write, new insights emerge or are clarified. I therefore reserve the right to go on growing in my understanding, and to even contradict myself in future writing. This book is an open invitation for you to join me in a journey of discovery.

1   The nature of the Eco-City

The City is of Night, perchance of Death,
But certainly of Night; for never there
Can come a lucid morning's fragrant breath
After the dewy morning's cold grey air.
James Thomson, 1880[1]

*We respond only to the problems of city life,
rarely to its potential.*
Kenneth Schneider[2]

Exchange not motion

The scene below of a Paris street provided the first key to unlocking a concept of an Eco-City. What captivated my attention was the seating arrangement. I had been used to seeing seats at outdoor cafes clustered *around* the table, but here, for the first time, I saw seats in straight lines, all facing out like seats in a theatre.

The Paris scene illustrates perfectly the centuries old European tradition of the street as a stage – the social and cultural epicentre of urban living. For hundreds of years the street has been the stage for music, processions, weddings, funerals, triumphal entry of kings and queens, education, public debate, prayer, commerce and theatre. In fact, when the first enclosed theatres were built in the sixteenth and seventeenth centuries, set-makers knew of only one appropriate backdrop – the street.[3]

It was not until I had shown a slide of this Paris street a few dozen times that I asked myself the question: 'What are these people really doing as they look at the faces of those walking past?' From my own experience I concluded that some were watching the drama of life played out in the faces of the passing parade. They were trying to read the stories etched into the faces of these real life actors. The clues to the story-line lay in the eyes, the posture, the gait, the mannerisms and dress. Some of the stories were simple one-act plays, others sagas of tragedy and triumph. For those on the chairs, it matters little how accurate these imagined real-life dramas are. This is an exercise in summoning up from

the dark cellars the high and low points of their own journey. It is a process that puts them in contact with their own history, connecting them to their own past. It is a way of clarifying their own dreams for the future; a therapeutic exercise which promotes emotional, psychological and spiritual well-being.

Why do we have cities?

By glimpsing this unseen *exchange* that is taking place between those on the seats and those on the street, we also catch a glimpse of the true meaning of the Eco-City: a place of exchange. Cities were invented to facilitate exchange of information, friendship, material goods, culture, knowledge, insight, skills, and also the exchange of emotional, psychological and spiritual support. This exchange is more difficult if people are scattered all over the countryside and do not have access to these exchange opportunities. That is why we build cities. Cities are a concentration of people and structures that enable mutual exchange to take place while minimising the travel needed.

People desire access to this rich diversity of exchange opportunities for their survival and for their growth as human beings. Cities are a recognition that, if we are to grow into our fullest potential, we need what other people can give us. The city is therefore an eco-system created by people for mutual enrichment. In an eco-system, such as a rainforest, everything is interrelated and interdependent. Each organism provides something which is essential for the life of other organisms and, in return, receives from other organisms those things essential for their own survival and well-being. Take any of these organisms away from the context of their eco-system and their growth will be stunted or their survival jeopardised. Similarly, the city is an eco-system where, through mutual exchange, we mature and are nurtured.

What then is the place of transportation within the city? Cities are, by their very nature, a concentration of exchange opportunities brought together to minimise the need for travel or movement. But even though the city's basic function is to maximise access to exchange opportunities while minimising the need to travel, a certain amount of travel or movement is still necessary within the city to facilitate mutual exchange. Hence the need for transport systems as a means to an end, to facilitate exchange.

The movement myth

In all of life there is a tendency to focus on means rather than ends. So for many people, movement, rather than facilitating exchange, has become the goal of transport. The reason for going has been forgotten. In a recent survey of engineers and planners almost two-thirds of them used concepts of movement in describing the basic function of transport.[4] This response should not surprise us. Not only is it a manifestation of the tendency for the means to become the end, it is also a reflection of a myth that pervades the whole of Western society. The myth? Freedom lies in motion. Many people assume that freedom of movement is the foundation stone of our democratic society. They think if you are free to move you are, by definition, free. But the ability to move does not necessarily equate with freedom. Ask any prisoner. They are free to run marathons around the perimeter of an exercise quadrangle, or walk around their cells to their hearts' content. Prison walls do not stop movement *per se;* they stop *access.* Or to be more accurate, they stop access to exchange opportunities. True freedom lies in having access to the interaction (exchange) that we need for personal and community well-being.

In fact, for many people movement can be an expression of tyranny; a loss of freedom. Take for example parents who are forced to drive their children to sporting events because the street has become too dangerous for spontaneous play. Both the parents and the children experience a loss of freedom, in spite of the fact that these extra trips will show up in the statistics as an increase in the average number of trips per person. As such, they will be hailed by planners and politicians as evidence of increased mobility which is assumed to equate to increased quality of life.

The parents are forced to make a trip which is of no intrinsic value and the children have lost a spontaneous socialising event. Besides, these parents' forced trips may also contribute to a loss of freedom for others. For example, these trips may help erode the play space of children in other streets, forcing even more parents to drive their children to organised activities. And if the roads these parents are forced to use are already full, this additional traffic may be the trigger for congestion.

Of course this myth of motion has deeper roots than just an association of motion and freedom. Motion, in Western thinking, is also tied to productivity and usefulness. An idle machine is an unproductive machine. A machine is only of value if it is moving and producing. Because we have reduced ourselves (and our cities) to the level of machines, we often judge our self worth by the pace at which we live. To be still is to be idle and to be idle is often seen to be a sin. Yet productivity and meaning in ecological terms has very little to do with motion *per se*. Productivity and meaning has to do with the richness of relationships within the eco-system – the sense of purpose that each element of the eco-system bestows by both giving and receiving from the other elements. That meaning is tied up in the realisation that if one element is taken out of the eco-system, the whole eco-system will be

poorer for its absence. In eco-system terms, even death – the ultimate state of non-motion – gives to a person a sense of meaning and productivity. The leaves that fall become the food of other plants, the home of micro organisms essential for the forest's well-being. And when the tree itself dies, it too becomes an essential part of the forest's ongoing life. Nothing is lost.

And here, again, we come face to face with the central focus of any eco-system and hence with the central focus of the city: interdependence and mutual exchange – not necessarily motion.

Events not matter

The Eco-City, along with all eco-systems, cannot be understood through a process of objectively looking at individual parts. It is impossible to understand the Paris street scene by taking one of the chairs into a laboratory and examining its molecular structure or ergonomic design.

Mechanistic thinking, which has dominated Western thought patterns for about the last 400 years, believes the universe is a machine which can be understood by dismantling it piece by piece and examining each individual element in isolation. Reality for modern science is matter; stuff which can be examined, measured and manipulated. This reductionist thinking (reducing everything to its base building blocks) led to the belief that knowledge could be divided into disciplines – areas of specialisation where 'experts' become the guardians of the knowledge gleaned from their examination of one base building block.

These experts would break this Paris street scene down into its constituent parts. The traffic engineer might examine what happened to the cars displaced from the space by the pedestrians and chairs. The urban planner might measure pedestrian flows and to what extent the chairs may impede this flow. The ergonomics engineer would be interested in the design of the chairs – do they offer maximum support for the statistically average-sized human frame? The molecular scientist would examine the structure and stability of the PVC molecules in the seats when exposed to ultra-violet radiation in the form of sunshine. The economist may want to know if people drink more or less coffee when seated in rows rather than clusters and how this would affect the GDP if all cafes seated their customers in straight rows.

Mechanistic thinking misses the *event* which is happening in this street because events or processes are not the stuff of science. How can you 'see' the silent story-telling going on in people's minds? How can you measure the creative energy this may generate? How can you quantify the healing of old emotional wounds that may be facilitated? The atoms and molecules that make up the chairs, the bitumen, the coffee in the mugs, are the most 'real' things in this scene. And for many the ultimate reality is the money paid for the coffee.

Mechanistic or reductionist thinking focuses on individual elements. On the other hand, those adopting an holistic or eco-relational view focus on the total event in all its richness. The event here is a set of relationships that express themselves in dynamic exchange. Eco-systems are understood by examining the complex web of internal relationships – in this case the relationships between the street, the chairs, the people on the street and the people using the chairs.

Eco-relational thinking, which Charles Birch refers to as the postmodern world view, or which others call the ecological world view, is not new. It was largely the way people viewed the world before Newton ushered in the scientific age. In Western culture there have been many great holistic thinkers. Writers such as Jane Jacobs[5] and Lewis Mumford[6] inspired me to learn the gentle art of watching a city scene in order to discern the 'event' – the intimate web of relationships and the exchange taking place between all elements. The ecological view has also been kept alive by many indigenous cultures and by many women who, through their nurturing role, have also preserved a 'relationship-oriented' as opposed to 'thing-oriented' view of the world.

Currently we are on the precipice of a revolution which Birch claims will have an even greater impact than the Scientific Revolution and the Enlightenment. He sums up the new insights of science which are fueling this revolution:

As we penetrate matter we don't find isolated building blocks but a complex web of relationships between the parts of a unified whole. The world can to some extent be divided into parts, but the notion of independent parts breaks down. The parts are defined by their interrelations.[7]

For example, in high school, students are shown pictures of atoms which look like planets revolving around a sun. In the case of hydrogen it is often explained that the single 'planet' is in fact an electron and the centre 'sun' is a single proton. What scientists know is that what is pictured in this representation is a snapshot of an event – electron and proton bound together in relationship (electron trying to speed off into space but captured by the attraction of the proton). If the relationship between these two elements ceases, the atom ceases to exist.

Nor can the atom be understood in terms of this snapshot because its nature is further determined by its wider context. When two hydrogen atoms and one oxygen atom enter into a relationship the result of their union is water. Water cannot be understood by individual examination of either a hydrogen or an oxygen atom. This is a dynamic relationship that produces the unpredictable.

In a similar way the same electron will perform very different functions in mud than it will in a brain. In the mud it may stay in a stable relationship to its nucleus for a million years. In the brain, however, it becomes part of an electrical impulse which leads to a creative thought which may ultimately change the course of human history.

So, even in basic science, the building blocks of atoms and electrons can only be truly understood if they are examined as part of a particular event which involves a particular set of dynamic relationships. The picture of the seats in Paris is not a picture of a street, some chairs, some people, and some pedestrians. It is a snapshot which represents an event consisting of a dynamic set of relationships. Similarly, the city or its transport system cannot be understood by looking at its individual parts, for example, home, work, cars and people.

Earlier I suggested that the central function of a city is exchange. I limited the understanding of exchange to exchange between humans of goods, information and psychological support. But this exchange may also take place between people and other elements such as seats or a sculpture. All elements in the city, whether they be chairs, streets, trees or rocks, can become part of a dynamic event and therefore part of a dynamic relationship.

Pro-city not anti-city

The process of trying to discern the dynamic events and relationships that give rise to what we can see and sense can open up surprising insights. Take for example the picture opposite of chairs in the Munich square. What struck me was that they are not nailed down. In my hometown, Brisbane, we would not dare leave loose chairs in the city square or mall. They would more than likely be stolen. This raises an obvious question. Why are the city fathers and mothers not frightened these Munich seats will be stolen? Part of the explanation may be that the people of Munich feel a strong sense of ownership towards the chairs. After all, you only steal something that belongs to someone else. In cities like Munich, one feels a strong sense of place. The Munich people appear to embrace their city as their home. These chairs are therefore an important manifestation of a relationship between Munich residents and their city.

A counter line of exploration is also opened up by these Munich seats. Why is there not the same sense of ownership in most Australian or US cities? Unlike Europeans, most Anglo-Saxons do not view the city as a hot-house in which great civilisations flourish, in which individuals are nourished and grow into their fullest potential. Many people in these countries do not even like their cities.

Robert Brambilla, in *More Streets for People*, argues that during the Industrial Revolution 'cities evolved from living places to places of work'.[8] While Brambilla blames the Industrial Revolution itself for the transition of cities from living places to work places, the seeds for this transition were sown much earlier in the Scientific Revolution of the sixteenth and seventeenth centuries.

The philosopher René Descartes is given much of the credit for systematizing the new values that emerged during this time. Physicist Fritjof Capra says that according to Descartes:

> ...the material universe was a machine and nothing but a machine. There was no purpose, life or spirituality in matter. Nature worked according to mechanical laws, and everything in the material world could be explained in terms of the arrangement and movement of its parts.[9]

Lewis Mumford comments:

> The ultimate result of this mechanistic doctrine was to raise the machine to a higher status than an organism...Thus a set of metaphysical abstractions laid the groundwork for a technological civilization, in which the machine in the latest of its many incarnations would in time become the Supreme Power.[10]

Indeed, the machines in the factories of the industrial city became a deity around which life revolved. Serving this new Supreme Power

became the central focus of life and as Brambilla so rightly observed, the city's focus changed from being a place for living and experiencing the unquantifiables of life – culture, intellectual stimulation, community, spirituality – to a place to work. The focus became the pursuit of quantifiables, the consumer goods which the new Supreme Power would impart to those who gave unyielding service and sacrifice.

But an even more fundamental change of focus resulting from the Industrial Revolution was the change in the way the city itself was viewed. Because 'the material universe was a machine and nothing but a machine' the city died as an organism and was transformed into a machine. The focus shifted from a passion for life to a passion for efficiency, productivity and profit. Previously people viewed the world, and hence their cities, holistically. Before the Industrial Revolution the universe had not yet been atomised or broken down into machine parts and the city had been viewed as an eco-system, almost a living organism.

When the city was viewed as a machine, people's function in the city changed from being a vital, indispensable link in the eco-system to being an anonymous and dispensable cog in the machine. People became the human fodder to work the great engines of the factories to produce the city's wealth. The unquantifiables (purpose, self-determination) which make people human were either denied or subjugated. Thus the housing for the factory workers of the industrial city became legendary with overcrowding, open sewers and rampant disease. The chief consideration was output.

One social reformer, who rightfully hated what he saw in industrial London, was the English court reporter Ebenezer Howard. Howard concluded that the only solution was to rescue the poor from their living hell by taking them out of London and resettling them in a Garden City where population and density would be strictly controlled and industry hidden in a discrete pocket screened from the residential area. Howard gave birth to a social reform movement – city planning. Both Howard's city planning movement and society in general adopted a view of the city as essentially an evil place. As Peter Hall observed in *Cities of Tomorrow*: 'Most of the philosophical founders of the planning movement continued to be obsessed with the evils of the congested Victorian slum city'.[11] Howard saw large gatherings of people at high densities as being inherently evil and that lowering densities was a means of improving the nation's moral and physical health.

Howard was not alone in his hatred of the overcrowded industrial revolution cities. Lord Alfred Tennyson, in his poem 'Maud', articulated what many felt when he wrote:

I loathe the squares and streets
And the faces one meets.

While Continental Europe also had an Industrial Revolution and saw its cities 'degraded', there seemed to remain deep in the European psyche a pro-urban bias which would not allow an abandonment of the city – or the *concept* of the city. Meanwhile, the Anglo-Saxon loathing of the city inspired millions to flee to the new frontiers of unlimited space in Australia and the US. In these countries, Howard's utopian vision of a 'Garden City' found fertile soil as his disciples tried to build cities in which every family enjoyed their own private plot of 'country' with industry kept well away. This utopian vision was made possible, first by the advent of public transport, then increasingly by the automobile.

Even today the city is often seen by Anglo-Saxons as a necessary evil, a place to be mined for consumer goods. Many people would not stay there if they had a choice. While Australia became the most urbanised nation, it hung on to a romantic view of the country and a certain loathing of the city. As Peter Newman writes:

> We have never really been committed to the city. We do not have a belief in the city as a positive force for good, a place where culture can grow and all that is best in the human spirit can thrive... In general the English, American and Australian traditions have been to idealise places that are rural and our literary heroes are from the countryside, the prairie, the bush. Cities only serve to corrupt the purifying aspects of country life.[12]

The lives of many people in Australia and the US have become subservient to the ritual of keeping the bush myth alive. Having staked a claim to a private plot of non-city, non-bush, people either sit in squatters chairs and dream of how one day they will emulate the rugged individualism of the early settlers and become self-sufficient on five hectares, just one hour's drive from the city, or they mark off the days to the next long weekend when they can climb aboard their escape machines and flee from the loathsome city to the peace and serenity of the bush. Ironically, the most popular camping sights are those where it is impossible even to walk between the tent ropes. People then sit on deck chairs around a lantern and experience the real joy of urban living, sharing with other human beings. According to Kenneth Schneider, 'The European rural tradition is psychologically urban and our urban tradition is psychologically rural'.[13]

This half-hidden loathing of the city is like a person with a poor self-image; they stuff their face and grow fat; drape themselves in ill-fitting clothes; disfigure and mutilate themselves as self-punishment; and become depressed, depressing and anti-social. The result? The LA riots. Like a person who is apathetic or despises their own body, city dwellers have also neglected the vehicle for the expression of their humanity and in some cases entered a phase of self-destruction. Yet this loathing of cities is a direct result of having denigrated both ourselves and our cities by rejecting our humanness and rejecting the city as one context in which our humanness can grow and mature.

These loose seats in Munich point to a different tradition; a different kind of relationship between city and citizen. As Professor Mähler of Munich's School of Architecture has said:

> Munich's pedestrian mall certainly was the first sign and a physical symbol for a new understanding of our city. This understanding views the city less as a functional structure and more as a *Lebensraum* [room for living] for human beings, that engages people emotionally in their city.[14]

Chaotic – not mono-cultural

One thing is obvious when you look at the seats in the Munich square: the space looks chaotic. Where is the guiding hand of a planner to bring order? There is no design, no straight lines, no symmetrical shapes, only chaos. But it is reminiscent of nature where plants are never seen growing in a neat row or laid out in symmetrical designs. Like nature this space is constantly changing, moving, and surprising. Chaotic yet brimming with life and creative energy.

Mechanistic thinkers hate disorder and diversity; their mission in life is to bring 'order'. While mechanistic thinking may hate disorder, nature is full of it. In the chaos of the upper atmosphere, nature produces billions of snowflakes, no two alike. In fact, both chaos and diversity are essential to the very survival of nature. It is from bio-diversity – the genetic pool – that new breeds and new life forms emerge which are able to survive a changing environment.

Chaos is absolutely essential for the emergence of new life forms. Chaos allows for the chance meeting of two previously unconnected elements which could not have met in a totally ordered world. When these two elements enter a relationship, the unpredictable may happen, like in the coming together of two gases to form water. The same process of chaos and diversity happens in creative thinking. The brain allows unrelated ideas to bounce off each other in a pool of chaos. Every now and then a connection is made between previously unrelated ideas and a creative thought is born which bears little or no resemblance to the original component parts. Diversity provides the pool of ideas and chaos the chance for them to meet. Both chaos and diversity are essential to life and therefore are inseparable from sustainability.

Mono-cultures, for example single crop farms, are inherently unstable. They must be sustained from outside with massive supplies of fertiliser, water and pesticides. Ironically, the farmer is fighting against nature's attempt to reassert its diversity. For nature, chaos and diversity are the life-link to the future. Could it be that those in the Western world are yet to learn that their survival depends on social and cultural diversity and tolerance of some chaos? Segregated, regimented, mono-cultural cities are socially, and in the long term economically, unsustainable.

Therefore, in the chaotic arrangement of the Munich chairs we can discern the opportunity for new levels of creative life to emerge. These chairs invite, almost command, people to exercise their creative freedom. As Jan Tanghe writes:

> It has all too often slipped our minds that a sense of fun and a large measure of irrationality can be as meaningful as the development of knowledge. The structures of attractive cities is sometimes very irrational by modern standards of efficient and rational planning, but the true values in life often seem to stem from the unforeseen and the unplanned. The best cities are like the best parties; nobody planned them in advance and that is why they are so successful.[15]

The tragedy of many modern, Western cities is that they have become mono-cultural. By mono-cultural I do not mean that they do not contain many cultures and a wide range of activities, but that these have been segregated and fenced off from each other much as a farmer may fence off different crops.

Suburbs are created for certain socio-economic groupings. Admission to the next 'higher' area is governed by earning capacity. To cap it off a 'privacy box' has been invented which allows them to move through public places in private, thus avoiding contact with others. The privacy box even allows them to spirit their children to mono-cultural sporting activities where they can play with children of the same age and from similar socio-economic groupings. It also allows children to be spirited to an educational institution befitting the aspirations of their parents.

This 'fencing' goes further. Our senior citizens are locked in old-age homes where they socialise with people of their own age. Or even worse, having stolen their socialising space for car movement, they are left stranded alone in their own homes. To ease society's social conscience they are given a *senior citizens'* bus to take them to a *senior citizens'* hall. Those with disabilities are also given special buses to take them to *sheltered* workshops. To add insult to injury the buses are labeled to indicate who is inside so they can be avoided.

Such a mono-cultural existence impoverishes all those in the city. One of the lessons learnt from the chairs is the importance of what may be considered the most insignificant elements in an eco-system. Chairs look dispensable, yet they are silent sentinels to the creative thoughts that were forged as people reclined upon them. Scientific breakthroughs, songs written, solutions found, friendships forged, resolutions made and self-respect reclaimed; all these experiences have enriched the city.

Therefore, the chair has played a significant part in making great cities what they are. Similarly we know the importance of the smallest element in other eco-systems. Remove one micro-organism from the soil in a rainforest and you may upset the entire balance of the eco-system and threaten its very survival.

The segregation of those who are elderly, young, disabled, poor or from a different ethnic background is not so much to their detriment, but to society's. These people have gifts to enrich the lives of others and society is the poorer for not having them. These gifts may not always be comfortable, and often they challenge prejudices and assumptions. They also throw a comfortable world into chaos. But as I have already suggested, it is chaos which provides the opportunity for worlds to clash, new relationships to form and new life forms to emerge. Such experiences are an essential part of the maturing and growing process.

This is also why it is essential we have eccentrics in our society. By definition an eccentric does not represent the status quo; they are 'off centre'. They are the disturbers of our peace and their role is indispensable. Every eccentric carries the potential future of the planet within them. Maybe the ideas or insights have already formed in the chaos of their mind. Or perhaps their world, colliding with ours, may form a relationship from which new life emerges.

A few years ago some Brisbane residents were fighting the establishment of a funeral parlour in their suburb. One person wrote to the paper complaining that this exposure to death would 'erode their quality of life'. My reply to the paper asked how living in a fool's paradise and segregating themselves from the realities of everyday life increase a person's quality of life? Surely some exposure to death would encourage people to make more sober judgements, prioritise their time more carefully or value their existing relationships more dearly. It would encourage them to build more humane cities that allowed for more compassion. Certainly the last thing we should do is tell those who mourn that we do not want to share their grief and that they must grieve in private.

Recently I interviewed a 45 year-old woman for a radio program. She was an epileptic and therefore had never been able to obtain a car licence. At first she thought having to raise two children without a car was a disability. But in the end she counted herself to be more privileged than car drivers and saw the car drivers as those with the handicap. She said:

> When you're on a bus and you're travelling out of peak hours, the biggest percentage of those on the bus are elderly. You see their struggle on and off the bus and the thing that dawns on you is, 'Gee, I'm getting older and one day I'll probably have arthritis and a walking stick'.

I'm seeing life as it is by travelling on public transport. I'm seeing a dimension of life that I'm forced to address. I think I'm very honoured because I face reality on a day to day basis. I'm not sure a lot of people are in contact with that any more.

John Roberts made the same observation: 'The vehicle also turns its occupants into disadvantaged persons, for it distracts them from the very activities that made cities happen: the face to face exchange of goods, services, information and ideas...' (Emphasis added).[16] Our world view becomes seriously distorted when we cut ourselves off from the significant others who are different from us.

This lesson was brought home to me with incredible force when I visited Groningen in the north of Holland. I was only there for three hours yet saw three people in wheelchairs using the streets or bike lanes. The scene of two young people taking an elderly blind man for a walk was particularly moving.

The significance of my Groningen experience did not hit me until I reflected on my visit to Los Angeles where I had walked the streets for six hours trying to interview people, without success. There appeared to be few middle-class white Americans left on the streets of Los Angeles. The streets had been abandoned to poor blacks, immigrant Mexicans and the down-and-outs. These people viewed with suspicion anyone who wanted to talk to them. It suddenly occurred to me that I could not recall seeing anyone in wheelchairs using the streets of Los Angeles. Nor could I recall seeing anyone using wheelchairs in Paris or during two days in London. In Groningen I realised that one of the most insidious side effects of car-based transport systems was its contribution to segregation and the loss of social diversity.

Spontaneous – not planned

I have suggested that maximising exchange and minimising travel were primary functions of the city. Also that some travel or movement is still necessary to facilitate this exchange. But is a trip always necessary to facilitate exchange?

The centre of Nuremburg, a city of 500,000 people in Germany, has five kilometres of pedestrianised streets. On my visit there in 1989 I was surprised to find that the city square, which was once full of parked cars, was now full of brightly coloured market stalls. Walking along the main street, which once carried 30,000 vehicles per day, I crossed a stone bridge which had more market stalls down one side. As I approached the other side of the bridge I could hear the lively laughter and playful screams of children. There, in a little side street beside the cathedral, I

discovered the Lobby for Children. People were handing out information about their activities and providing entertainment for children. At the front of the cathedral stood an Indian band entertaining a large crowd of onlookers. Inside the cathedral were people sitting in meditative silence, awed by the majestic architecture. Fifty metres up the street were other professional musicians, again playing ethnic music. A little further along people sat around the base of a monument in the centre of the street, some reading and some watching the passing parade. One hundred metres on was a sculpture fountain which depicted a dramatic interpretation of a famous poet's ode to the ups and downs of married life. People would stand for anything up to an hour, gradually moving around the fountain, studying every detail, possibly identifying the various stages of their own marital relationship.

Twelve months after my return to Australia, and after viewing the slides I had taken in this street numerous times, it suddenly dawned on me that what I had observed was the real basis of city life: exchange. I had witnessed the exchange of goods, information, culture, friendship and inspiration. But all of this exchange was taking place *in* the street, as opposed to our understanding of streets as devices for taking us *to* destinations. In other words, the people of Nuremburg were not only using their streets for going to places; the streets were places – places which gave them access to a diverse range of exchange opportunities.

What struck me about these exchanges taking place in the street was that they were spontaneous. In making a trip for some other purpose citizens could encounter a market stall that was not there the day before;

come across a community action group they did not know existed; stop to listen to a busker they did not know would be there; bump into an old friend with whom they had lost contact; or just stop to reflect in front of the fountain for ten minutes and gain new inspiration. These exchanges were largely unplanned and spontaneous.

It was then I realised that there were two ways to gain access to exchange opportunities: planned access and spontaneous access. Planned access is when we make a deliberate trip – perhaps to the doctor, the shop, or to pay a bill. Spontaneous access is when unplanned exchanges happen in the course of a planned trip. It was this simple realisation that formed the basis of a paper presented to the International Transport Conference in 1991. My paper had been printed but not yet delivered when I discovered a third type of access: home-based access.

I was preparing for a radio program on streets and decided I would interview some of the senior citizens in my suburb, Ashgrove, in Brisbane. In exploring the role of the street in the life of the neighbourhood my attention was quickly drawn to the issue of home deliveries. There was a time when everything was delivered: fish, bread, cakes, groceries, milk, kerosene, and ice. The order-man would call in the morning and the groceries would be delivered that afternoon. Competition was so great that grocers would go door to door trying to persuade people to give them a trial for one month. Some people would give different grocers alternating months. The service was comprehensive. As one person commented:

> We used to get the groceries delivered, and the butcher used to come round in his truck, and you'd go out and he'd cut your meat while you were there. The fruit man used to come round. The milkman used to come round. The bread man used to come round. The whole lot. Everything you wanted in the house...

For these old-timers home deliveries had a distinct advantage:

> Well you didn't have to go out. You didn't have to go and have a bath and get dressed up or anything like that to go to the shops... You'd just go out to the vehicle, get what you want and you were home...

In fact there was a very strong link between home-based exchanges and spontaneous exchanges.

> They [the neighbours] would gather around [the delivery cart] and have a yarn and you'd say, 'Oh, what's the time?' 'Nine o'clock.' 'Ah well, we'll go into Mrs. Jackson's for a cup of tea.' And you'd go into Mrs. Jackson's for a cup of tea and you'd find two or three more of your neighbours in Mrs. Jackson's – just dropped in for a cup of tea.

Neither was the exchange between the grocer and residents just a matter of exchange of goods and money.

> Everybody had their weekly accounts at the grocers...and you'd go down to pay the account and you'd finish up with a little bag of lollies for paying it.

Even for kids, the delivery man was an important part of the social interaction between adults and children.

> Yes, we used to have open run, and follow the baker's cart around and sit on the back and have a free ride and if you had sixpence you bought a few cakes off the cake man...

> I remember the fruiterer coming around, and that was a big event down the street. He always sung out to us and we used to ask for a few specks to get by and he'd always call out, 'Praise the Lord', and 'Hallelujah' was our reply. He was a great salvationist. But, yeah, the good old days...

Some people may argue that a planned trip is involved in home deliveries because the delivery van comes to the customer. But there are two significant differences. Firstly, the exchange opportunity is brought to the people – not vice versa. Secondly, the planned trip is atomised so as to be almost insignificant. For one person to gain access to the bread on the van and the smile of the delivery man, the delivery van must only travel the width of one or two house blocks. What we are establishing is that there are a variety of ways in which people gain access to exchange opportunities and as I will show later, some are far more efficient than others.

Home-based exchange is not just restricted to home deliveries. Telephones and tele-commuting (working from home via computer terminal) are also forms of home-based exchange. And so are the interactions which once took place between people sitting on their front verandah or steps and the people who walked by on the footpath which was once considered an extension of people's living space. A 45 year-old woman recalled the following scenes from Wooloongabba in Brisbane.

> In the hot summer days kids would be running around, often in just underpants and a singlet because of the heat, and we'd play hopscotch or hoops on the footpath. We often played together because we had little yards and there was a strong sense of community involvement. We often played in the cool of the evening when it was still light, and I can remember that one of the daily activities of my mother was to shell the peas or string the beans... So she'd sit outside on the steps with a piece of newspaper, a colander, and her greens. She'd be there for the local people passing by and she'd have regular *exchange*. I'd be there some-times listening in to the conversations. And it was just taken for granted that there was always somebody going to be passing by. There was that community spirit. (Emphasis added)

While most people in auto-cities have lost sight of spontaneous and home-based access, which supplied so many of the exchange needs before the advent of the car, they have also lost sight of how much the 'self-contained' neighbourhood (lots of facilities close by) contributed to giving their forbears higher levels of exchange – without need for cars. For example, in the Ashgrove interviews I found that not only did the suburb once have an abundance of corner stores, but there was also a picture theatre and a Progress Hall where dances were held every Wednesday and Saturday night. In the words of one old-timer, 'Saturday night was the big one'.

> My mother and father were very good dancers. Everyone used to take their kids up, even babies. They used to put the babies in a room, and they'd just pop in and see if they were asleep. Between dances kids like myself used to slide up and down the floor, pull one another along the floor...

I asked, 'So you didn't need baby sitters to go out?' The reply was, 'No, I never heard of baby sitters when I was a kid. If we went out we all went out together'.

It was apparent that older people enjoyed incredibly high levels of exchange in spite of the spread-out nature of Australian cities and the low levels of car ownership. A striking feature of the interviews I conducted with older people was their acceptance of the 'time equals progress' myth. The first question I would ask was how the streets had changed over time. Many responded that the streets had changed for the better and it was great to be able to drive around wherever they wanted. They could not imagine how the city could cope without cars.

Yet after questioning them about how they related to the street as children, their ability to explore the neighbourhood in safety, home deliveries, levels of community interaction in the street, the corner stores and the locally supplied forms of entertainment, I would often pose the same question I had started with, 'Do you think the changes are for the best?' Invariably, those who had enthused about the march of progress suddenly changed their minds. Sure, the car had opened up new possibilities for weekend trips to the beach, but as they reflected on the cost of that new freedom, they realised that the spontaneous exchange they had lost was far greater than the new destinations they had gained.

I have already hinted at the link between spontaneous, home-based exchange and diversity. Spontaneous exchange, by its very nature, is chaotic; you have no control over who or what you may encounter. It is the opposite of a planned exchange where you choose beforehand the place, the time, and the nature of the exchange. It is only out of spontaneous exchange – the encounter that lies outside of present experience and knowledge – that yet undreamed of possibilities arise.

And like amino acids forming in a shallow sea billions of years ago, who knows what new levels of life may evolve from these accidental, unplanned encounters.

Because the car kills off opportunity for spontaneous exchange it also kills off diversity and thus aborts the opportunity for new relationships, new ideas and new cultural experiences. The 45 year-old epileptic woman who counted her carless condition as a great asset, became convinced that she was privileged after the following incident:

> I'll give you an example of how I met one of the local people in this street. He was an elderly Greek man and he'd go down to the Greek shop to get some Greek bread and I met him on the bus. We formed a nice little friendship and we'd walk back together from the bus station to his house and I'd continue my journey. Then one day, while walking, I met another person in the neighbourhood and found out that the Greek man had died.

> I was very concerned about his widow. I went there one day and she was so lovely. With very limited language she invited me in for tea. I shared in a very beautiful way – very limited in a verbal sense – but there was a sharing of people and spirit. I was able to hold her and I was able to tell her what a lovely man her husband was. And I felt very honoured that through me knowing her husband, I knew that she was now a widow.

> If I hadn't met him on the bus I wouldn't have known him and I wouldn't have known she was now a widow. And it was through contact on a bus. Now if I'd been in a car, I would never have met him, her and the other people I've met through walking…or at the bus station. So that is an enrichment of my life and of my local community.

> Now if you're in a car you haven't got a chance to have a five minute chat, to hear a human voice, to acknowledge people's humanness. When we lose that, what are we? Robots?

The car not only allows us to build mono-cultural cities – it also kills off the essential spontaneity and life of the city.

Places not destinations

What is it that makes a *space* become a *place*, that magical something that we might call 'placeness'? There are ten ingredients of placeness,[17] one or more of which must be present for a space to be a place. In exploring these ingredients of placeness it becomes obvious why both the mechanistic city and traffic destroy places and turns them into 'destinations'.

- ■ Changes 'Mode of Being'
  Henry and Suzanne Crowhurst Lennard describe the 'shift in the mode of being' as a subtle shift from a future-oriented 'mode of becoming'

to a 'mode of being in the present'.[18] This shift in mode of being changes us from pre-programmed automaton to self-determinant person; alive and interacting with the immediate environment at the immediate moment. Placeness awakens within us an acute consciousness of the present 'event' and our relationship within that event.

The machine city is pre-occupied with output; a future state. Speed is an attempt to beat time and bring the future forward. It reinforces our future-oriented 'mode of becoming' because the focus of the journey is the activity (yet in the future) which we are rushing to. Speed also destroys the opportunity to experience the immediate environment at the immediate moment and divorces us from place. Schneider explains:

> The point about time and speed that our civilization has yet to understand is that both can annihilate experience, that is, rob experience of absorption, reflection, inner organization, reformulation of thought and behavior, and, ultimately, human meaning. Behavior that is rushed, rigidly paced or constantly pressed for greater output easily becomes barren of social worth or robbed of interpersonal feeling... The compulsive goer loses touch with the reasons for going, the doer with the reasons for doing.[19]

On the other hand walking and cycling, while still taking us to the future activity, allow us to experience the places we pass through in the present.

■ Provides opportunity to be 'addressed' by others
Place provides the opportunity for us to become aware of other people and for them to 'address' us. Their age, manner of dress, physical

attributes, ethnic origin, or social status, force us to conduct an internal dialogue. Hence the 45 year-old epileptic woman told how seeing elderly people struggling on and off buses forced her to deal with the fact that she herself was growing older.

In a similar way a child's laugh may cause us to reflect on our own childhood, or on what kind of world we are going to leave the children of the future. A child's cry of pain may remind us of the unresolved pain we experienced in our own childhood and cause us to deal with our own suppressed feelings. The staggering drunk may raise prejudices that frighten us and force us to explore why such feelings are present. Alternatively, we may ask ourselves how we would feel in their shoes. The story we tell of their lives deepens our wells of compassion and understanding.

When auto-cities allow people to enter public places in private (via the car) they destroy this element of placeness because the occupants can no longer address others, or be addressed themselves.

- Provides opportunity to be addressed by the physical environment
Most people have experienced a moment when a sculpture, fountain, inscription on a historical plaque, the autumn leaves on the ground, the song of a bird, the texture of a rock, or a weathered piece of wood have triggered a line of thought which has opened up new insight and new understanding. I have already described how the placement of chairs in Paris or Munich 'taught' me lessons.

Speed excludes us from experiencing the places we travel through, and hence excludes the opportunity for the elements of that place to address us. Road infrastructure also tends to obliterate many of the elements of place which could address us; creeks, parks, or intimate spaces. Besides, it is very hard to hear what a tree may be 'saying' to us while a huge truck rumbles past!

- Encourages fantasy and play
Lewis Mumford, quoting Dutch historian J. Huizinga, argues that play rather than work is the formative element in human culture and that humanity's most serious activity belongs to the realm of make-believe:

> Long before he had achieved the power to transform the natural environment, man had created a miniature environment, the symbolic field of play, in which every function of life might be re-fashioned in a strictly human style; as in a game.[20]

Mumford goes on to explain the importance of fantasy in humanity's development:

> In the dream world, space and time dissolve: near and far, past and future, normal and monstrous, possible and impossible merge into a hopelessly disordered conglomeration... Yet from the dream man got his first hint

that there is more to his experience than meets his eye... If man had not encountered dragons and hippogriffs in dream, he might never have conceived of the atom.[21]

Fantasy and play allow us to explore realms beyond immediate reality. We know that in children this play is a way of practising social and motor skills needed for survival in later life. But such play should not stop for adults. In fantasy and play we explore the past and shape a world not yet manifest. Fantasy and play are the essential ingredients of self determination. Without them we become pre-programmed automatons.

> Play is a relationship with reality which is not in the first place decided by the necessities of life, is not trapped within any financial or productivity relationships, but which finds its interest and fulfilment within itself. It is an open relationship with reality – creativity and spontaneity. Experience gained in play is decisive for awareness later on, for the pattern of one's reactions and the capacity to deal with the unknown. The serious world of grown-ups – where 'everything must be done' – is put in perspective in play.[22]

Placeness must encourage this sense of fantasy and play for all ages. It may be in the form of sculptures, the building forms, story-telling, community art, festivals, or seats where we can watch the passing parade and write our own dramas.

In the hustle and bustle of the mechanical city there is no time for fantasy and play. The last bastion for this fantasy and play have become cars themselves; the dream machines. They encourage the fantasy that time and space can be beaten, or that cars somehow enhance the power and prestige of the drivers. But these are negative fantasies that have no connection to eventual reality. They draw us into a fool's paradise and lull us into a false sense of security.

■ Encourages ecstatic exuberance

Henry and Suzanne Crowhurst Lennard describe the way place encourages ecstatic exuberance as follows:

> Sometimes, in the best of public places, and during certain occasions – celebrations and festivals, religious, traditional, civic, etc. – we step into another world that theologians and philosophers describe as 'ecstatic' mode, into the timeless experience of pure joy. Persons may sing or dance or become overwhelmed by the beauty of human and aesthetic experience.[23]

Such experiences are not always in the demonstrative excesses of celebration. They may roll over us whilst sitting by a stream and listening to the babble of the water; or whilst looking at a rock and contemplating its history. The trigger may be witnessing a kind deed; listening to music; the laugh of a child or the beauty of an aged and weathered face. These ecstatic experiences are essential for our psychological and spiritual well-being. They are moments when we cease to take ourselves seriously and reach out to touch the mystical 'something'.

■ Preserves a sense of mystery and adventure
Placeness hides its hand. It calls us back with promises of more. It reveals the picture slowly and tells a never-ending story. Placeness teases us and involves us in the unfolding drama. It draws us along. Thus a winding path or street forever changes the borders of the picture; with every step the elements in the picture take up new positions.

However, there is no mystery or unfolding drama in a modern, engineered road. The rule here is the straightest line between two points to facilitate the greatest speed. Kilometre after kilometre the picture frame never changes. The cost of every straight road is not only the places it destroys but the very essence of placeness itself.

■ Connects us to reality
A place connects us to reality. A small graveyard in the centre of a town is a constant reminder of our mortality. It breaks us out of our fantasy and makes us face the world as it really is. Placeness puts on display both the negative and positive sides of our humanity. As we discussed earlier, it helps us meet face to face our prejudices while at other times filling us with compassion and deep feelings of connectedness to humanity and the 'goodness' of the universe.

There may seem to be a contradiction between this aspect of placeness and the encouragement of fantasy, play and ecstatic exuberance. But in a real sense all of the above do connect us back to reality. In fantasy and play we deal with the past and begin shaping the future, both of which affect how we are to live in the present moment.

■ Provides links to the past
Places always have a story to tell. Some of these stories are historical stories, owned by the entire populace. Others are personal stories. For one person a tree may become a sacred site. Here as a child they may have played and climbed and eaten the fruit of the tree. Here love may have first blossomed and initials been carved in the trunk. Here they may have watched their own children climb with the noisy chatter and laughter touching the child within. Here, beneath the branches, they may have spread the ashes of their parents. Places are rich in memories – both joyous and painful – and they never tire of retelling their stories.

- Facilitates spontaneous exchanges
Place is space where people give and receive. As seen already these exchanges are not necessarily of a material nature, nor need they be overt. The mere presence of another is enough sometimes to provide comfort – emotional, psychological and spiritual support – or to trigger ideas and feelings that lead to new insight and understanding.

- Affirms people's identity
According to Martin Buber, the basis of human society is twofold, 'the wish of every person to be confirmed as to what he or she is, even as to what he or she may become, by other persons' and 'the innate capacity in human beings to confirm their fellow human beings in this way'. He goes on to suggest that 'actual humanity exists only where this capacity unfolds'.[24]

Placeness not only provides the opportunity for this mutual affirmation via the exchange of 'gifts', but in itself affirms people's identity by giving them a history and a future.

The tragedy of our modern cities is that we have destroyed placeness. We have turned places into destinations or converted them into movement corridors. We have forgotten that transportation can be more than just a means of getting to a place; it can be an experience of place itself. As Dan Burden puts it:

> If we think about it, transportation is more than getting there; it's what we discover along the way, including ourselves. It's the memories we freeze in our minds. It forms our character, our being, our very substance. As we get back in tune and in touch with planet earth, we learn of its spirit. That spirit pervades our own soul and we become whole and complete.[25]

Every person must have access to places which together provide all the above aspects of placeness. If not, the city and its inhabitants will suffer what environmental psychologist Mayer Spivak termed 'setting deprivation'.[26] Spivak gives an extreme example of how setting deprivation affects our mental state. When mental patients are placed in a restricted environment the setting deprivation further aggravates their illness – which causes them to be placed in more restrictive surroundings until they are eventually transferred to a ward for the intractably ill.

Loss of placeness and setting deprivation affect most people. So many cities are barren and artless, barbaric in the extreme and lacking any of the hallmarks of culture and civilisation. Worst of all is what is happening to children. Changing streets from 'places' to 'movement corridors' robs children of the opportunity to explore their neighbourhood in ever increasing circles as they mature. This freedom to explore the local neighbourhood is probably the key ingredient in children developing a feeling that they belong to a neighbourhood, a place. It not only gives them an opportunity to develop relationships with people of all ages who live in their neighbourhood, it gives them an opportunity to develop a relationship with the placeness of their physical environment. Robbing children of a sense of place robs them of the very essence of life.

> There was once a time when every child could gain experience (every day and near home) of what work – school – shopping – playing – fighting – being together – living and dying, really mean. This was experience of the richness of human experience – or as Tellegen called it: 'the wholeness of life'.[27]

Fracturing the relationship between children and their neighbourhood and physical environment results in increasing feelings of insecurity and increasing acts of violence towards both the community and the physical environment from which they have been alienated. Joseph Lyford, talking of New York city, said:

> Later on, when children born clean, ready and expectant, begin to malfunction and cause trouble, hundreds of millions of dollars are appropriated to have special teachers and policemen and youth workers build special classrooms and prisons and mental institutions, and finance hospital beds to get these children under control. The children who do survive this tempering process become adults, but in my neighbourhood an adult is a dead child.[28]

The alienation of children is further reinforced by what they do instead of exploring and socialising. For many these activities have been replaced by hours spent in front of the television where they can be passive observers of shows like *Sesame Street*, a make believe street where children play safely and go exploring; a street where there is exciting interchange between friendly neighbours; a street where traffic is never seen and as the theme song says 'the air is clean and sweet'. But they never have the opportunity to see how all this can actually work in real life. In this way we train adults whose only experience of community life is via a fantasy machine that produces soap operas with titles such as *Neighbours*. For these people, placeness, with its ten key ingredients, has become a fantasy which is permanently divorced from reality.

2

How traffic destroys
the Eco-City

*The pedestrian remains the largest single obstacle to
free traffic movement.*
Los Angeles planning report.[1]

*You can draw any kind of pictures you like on a clean
slate and indulge your every whim in the wilderness in
laying out a New Delhi, Canberra or Brasilia, but
when you operate in an overbuilt metropolis you have
to hack your way with a meat axe.*
Robert Moses, City Construction
Coordinator for New York, 1964[2]

*Spreading cities in every country march across the
globe devouring half a million acres of land every day.*
Peter Newman, Associate Professor,
Murdoch University, Western Australia[3]

Hey, this is toad turf

In 1935 the cane toad was imported into northern Queensland from Hawaii to combat a pest, the grey-backed beetle, which was affecting sugar cane crops. The cane toad had little effect on the beetle and within a short time had itself become a pest, spreading throughout the entire State and, eventually, into New South Wales. Recently my children, along with thousands of other Brisbane children, were asked by the council and State government to become 'Toad Busters'. Schools were encouraged to join in toad busting nights in Brisbane Forest Park. The toad had become a pest because it had upset the balance in the existing eco-system. Native frogs and other wildlife were disappearing because the delicate web of interrelationships that existed before the arrival of the toad was suddenly disrupted.

In a similar way the sudden injection of the car into the delicate web of relationships that constitute the Eco-City upsets a balance which had evolved over thousands of years. Because planners and engineers have viewed the city as a machine for the production of goods and the street as a machine for the movement of traffic, they have assumed that actions such as widening a road, allowing a regional shopping centre, or allowing unrestrained car use in the city would have linear, predictable results. But of course they do not. The city is a complex, dynamic eco-system where disruption of the balance in one set of relationships, affects the balance in all the others. Like the frogs in Brisbane, some things may even begin to disappear. What are the effects of introducing cars into the urban eco-system?

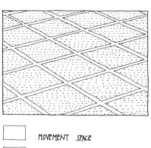

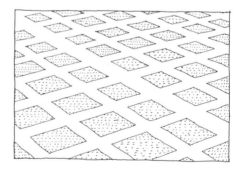

☐ MOVEMENT SPACE

▦ EXCHANGE SPACE

Fig. 1: How increasing movement space erodes exchange space which demands the city spread to compensate for the lost exchange opportunities.

Competition for space

Space in a city can be divided into two broad categories: exchange space (homes, shops, work places, parks, community halls, etc.) and movement space (roads, car parks, train tracks, walkways, etc.) used as a means of getting to exchange space. Increasing the amount of movement space requires transforming space from exchange space to movement space (see fig. 1). So to build a new road in an urban area, widen an existing road or build a car park, usually requires tearing down houses, work-places, community halls, or ripping up park or bushland. This conversion of space can also happen in an unseen way when the method of travel changes. Some space, for example the main street of Nuremburg, has a dual role; both movement and exchange. This was also true for the streets of Groningen where the streets were being used for both movement and social interaction. But if 30,000 cars were allowed to charge through the Nuremburg street or the streets of Groningen, this dual role would become a single role, converting the exchange dimension into a movement function (see fig. 2).

What happens then when exchange space is overtly or covertly converted to movement space? Well some of it is replaced on the city fringe. Valuable farmland or irreplaceable nature assets on the fringe of the city are converted into residential areas, shopping centres or work places. But much of the exchange opportunity can never be replaced. The spontaneous exchange is gone forever, as have the historic buildings, parks or even good friends.

This has a twofold result. Firstly, the city, and therefore the people, are poorer because they have some exchange opportunities obliterated.

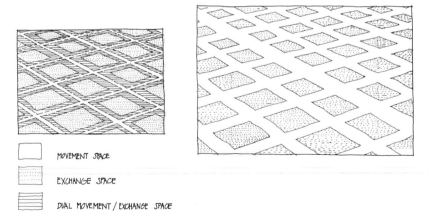

☐ MOVEMENT SPACE

▢ EXCHANGE SPACE

▤ DUAL MOVEMENT / EXCHANGE SPACE

Fig. 2: How converting dual purpose exchange/movement space to exclusively movement space erodes exchange opportunities and demands the city spread.

43

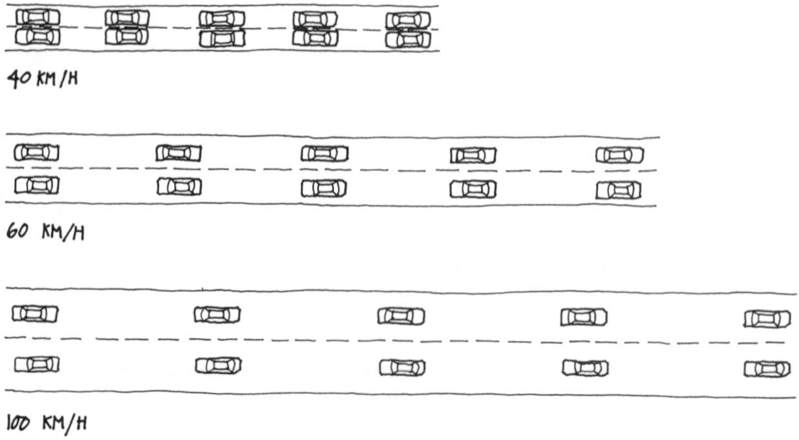

40 km/h

60 km/h

100 km/h

Fig 3: As traffic increases its speed it requires greater buffer zones front, back and side which requires greater space to move the same number of cars.

Secondly, they must travel further to reach the remaining exchange opportunities which are now spread over a greater area. This requires more movement which demands that more space be converted from exchange space to movement space, and so on. Even the motor vehicle industry understands this self-perpetuating cycle where new roads generate their own traffic which demands even more road space. In 1967 the *Asphalt Institute Quarterly*, the publication for oil and highway interest groups, stated:

> Every new mile tacked onto the paved road and street system is accompanied by the consumption of about 50,000 additional gallons of motor fuel a year. That's a total of 2.25 billion additional gallons of fuel use, accounted for by the added 45,000 miles of new roads built each year... In short, we have a self perpetuating cycle, the key element of which is new paved roads. The 45,000 new miles added to the road network each year accommodate automotive travel, generate fuel consumption, produce road building revenue. Scratch the new roads and the cycle ceases to function.[4]

This 'spreading-city syndrome' is compounded even further by the space demands of the car. Cars can take up to thirty times more space to move each person than public transport. Ironically, the faster traffic moves, the greater the space it demands (fig. 3). Not only does faster traffic require a greater buffer front and back, it also requires a greater buffer on either side.

The car also requires greater amounts of space for storage. A car consumes 20 times the space needed to park a bike. Legs stay with their owner and require even less storage space. Because cars must have numerous car spaces that lie idle for long periods of time (at home, workplace, shopping centre, pre-school, church, recreational facilities, etc.), the family car consumes about three times more space than the average family home.

It may be argued that countries like the United States, Canada and Australia have unlimited space so the spreading-city syndrome is not such a problem. The question is not whether space is limited or unlimited; it is, when does a city cease to be a city? For the record the USA has already paved two per cent of its entire land mass and ten per cent of all arable land.[5] Cities, by definition, are a concentration of diverse people, goods and facilities within a limited area, brought together in order to widen the possibility of choice while reducing the need to travel. One thing is therefore certain: keep spreading the same number of people over a larger and larger area and eventually you will no longer have a city. You have what Mumford calls an 'anti-city'.

It is the rich diversity and concentration of culture, information, institutions, public places, bushland and, above all, people that give a city vitality and interest. The relationships between these elements, concentrated together in one place, constitute the heart and soul of a city. Dilute their diversity and concentration and you begin to destroy the soul of the city. Thus the loss of one piece, for example an historic building, devalues all that is left.

History is now showing us the end results of a policy of converting living space into road space to solve congestion. Spreading cities not only end up with worse traffic problems; they are also terribly inefficient, costing increasing amounts to service with water, electricity, sewerage, drainage and roads. Residents are forced to pay an increasing share of their income to maintain their city. In an era of dwindling resources it is doubtful whether spreading cities like Los Angeles will be sustainable in the long term. But the greatest challenge is not purely economic survival. It is social and cultural survival.

Natural eco-systems exhibit a drive toward internal efficiency; maximum internal exchange for minimum use of resources. Take, for example, the human body's own blood system. Blood and the blood vessels are the movement infrastructure of the body; they also facilitate exchange. This system is so efficient that in most tissue, no cell is ever more than three or four cells away from a blood vessel. In Western cities, movement systems currently occupy one-third to one-half of total city area. Yet the human body's movement system (blood vessels and blood) takes up just five per cent of the body's volume.

It must be stressed again that I am not arguing for the abolition of cars *per se*. What I am saying is that in the Eco-City their use for most movements is not only inefficient but downright destructive. Cars feed on the very elements that make the city a city. Some people may argue that increasing road space gives residents greater mobility thus increasing the quality of their living by giving them access to a greater range of exchange opportunities – for example, a greater choice of job opportunities. At first glance this sounds like a convincing argument. But it ignores three factors:

- The spreading-city syndrome
  In the late nineteenth century, only a minority spent more than half an hour walking to work.[6] One hundred years later (1971), the average journey to work by car was 30 minutes and for those using public transport, slightly higher. Between 1901 and 1971 average journey length went from 3–4 kilometres to 10–11 kilometres in Melbourne and Sydney, while average speed of public transport and private cars remained constant or declined. The average speed of motor vehicles in Australian cities has not increased significantly since they were first mass produced in the 1920s. The spreading city has thus eaten up the gains of increased reach.[7]

- Loss of close-to-home job opportunities due to cross-commuting
  While a new freeway may give some people (those with access to a car) a greater area over which they can range when looking for a job, the freeway also encourages a gross inefficiency in the form of *cross-commuting*. Here is an example of how 'improving' the road infrastructure encourages greater inefficiencies in the form of cross-commuting. Tom lives in a suburb called Acorn and is looking for a

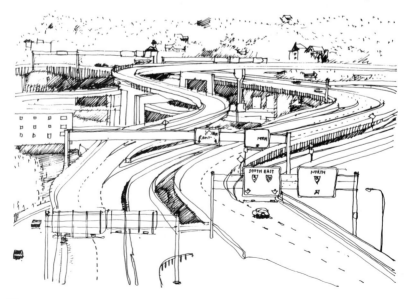

job as a service station attendant. Tom sees a position advertised at Zenna, a suburb 35 kilometres away. At first he dismisses the idea of applying but then realises that a new bypass has just been built that would have him there in 30 minutes, if he had a car. He decides to apply and if he is given the job he will buy a cheap bomb to get him there. He gets the job. That same afternoon, Freda who lives in Zenna finds herself unemployed and starts looking for a job as a service station attendant. She sees a job advertised at a place which is just 200 yards from where she lives. She rings up but finds that the job has just been filled by Tom. A week later she sees a job advertised in Acorn. Freda decides she will apply because the new bypass means she can probably be there in 30 minutes. She is given the job and so Tom and Freda pass each other every morning on the bypass, both going to a job within walking distance of each other's homes. So while the bypass increased the area over which Tom could range to find a job, it removed the freedom for Freda to work close to home and thus encouraged a gross inefficiency.

According to Patrick Moriarty and Clive Beed, who surveyed commuting patterns in Sydney, Melbourne, Adelaide and Perth, cross-commuting doubles the amount of travel really necessary. They concluded that 'nearly half of all commuter travel is unnecessary'.[8] Ian Manning showed similar results when he found that 71 per cent of people could find work in their local region yet in Sydney only 38 per cent did and in Melbourne only 33 per cent.[9] Manning also estimated that two-thirds of people could find employment within three or four kilometres (walking or cycling distance) of their home if distance was the over-riding factor in job selection. It must be noted that these figures are for existing auto-dominated cities. Much greater savings of travel would be feasible if the road space freed up by this halving of commuter traffic were then converted to job opportunities even closer to home.

Those who wish to argue that roads have given greater accessibility may quote from the numerous studies which show that the number of trips people make are increasing. These studies overlook two important factors. Firstly, most traditional trip studies did not count walk and cycle trips as trips. So trips like walks to the corner store, which did not show up in a previous trip survey, suddenly show up as drives to a regional shopping centre in later studies.

Secondly, these trip studies overlook the purpose of the trip and whether that purpose was fulfilled previously in some other way which did not require travel. For example, parents may record four extra trips a week driving their children to sporting activities. But is this a benefit when ten years ago these same children could play cricket and tennis in their own street or at a neighbourhood park?

Other trips may be forced simply to replace other exchanges that once happened spontaneously in the street. Many of these extra trips are induced trips with no net gain in quantity or quality of activity at the journey's end. For example, it may be argued that we now eat out more, but we must ask why we feel the need to eat out more. Could it be that this socialising activity is needed because traffic has eroded so many other opportunities for socialising in the neighbourhood? And, as I shall show later, the disturbing fact is that those who are able to increase their trips (in the vain attempt to maintain existing levels of exchange) are those who have access to a car. Those who do not are going backwards even faster with each increase in road infrastructure.

The growing zone-of-influence

Cars not only take over the space they need for moving, they also have a *zone-of-influence* which expands as speed and quantity of traffic increases. This means that the car not only demands that exchange space be converted to road or parking space, it also reduces or destroys the

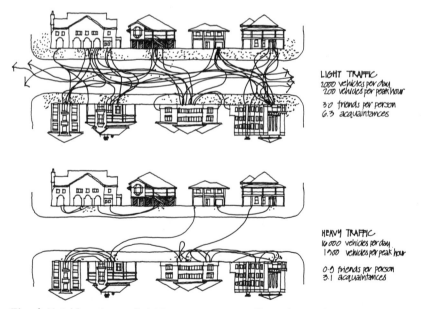

Fig. 4: Neighbouring and visiting on two streets: lines show where people said they had friends or acquaintances; dots show where people are said to gather. (Adapted from D. Appleyard, *Livable Streets.*)

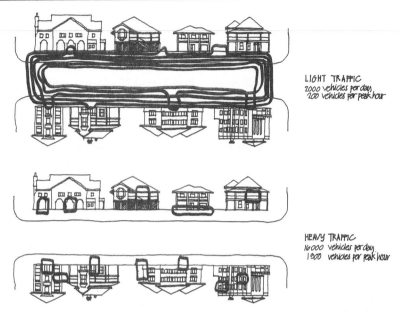

LIGHT TRAFFIC
2000 vehicles per day,
200 vehicles per peak hour

HEAVY TRAFFIC
16000 vehicles per day
1900 vehicles per peak hour

Fig. 5: Home territory on two streets: lines show areas people indicated as their 'home territory'. (Adapted from D. Appleyard, *Livable Streets*.)

effectiveness of exchange space.

In 1970, Donald Appleyard conducted a very interesting study in San Francisco.[10] He chose three residential streets which, on the surface, looked alike but which had different levels of traffic. He then carried out one hour interviews with 12 residents from each block, conducted as a survey on what it was like to live on their street and seeking suggestions for improvement. Residents were not told that Appleyard's primary interest was the effects of traffic on neighbourhood life. Appleyard supplemented the questionnaire with detailed observations and mapping of activities in each street.

The first street carried 2,000 vehicles per day and was referred to in the study as Light street. The second carried 8,000 vehicles per day and was called Medium street. The third carried 16,000 vehicles per day and was called Heavy street. Appleyard asked the residents to indicate where friends and acquaintances lived on a map of their street. The results showed that those on Light street had three times more friends and twice as many acquaintances as the people on Heavy street (fig. 4).

He also asked them to draw on the map of their street the area they considered to be their 'home territory'. Fig. 5 shows the 12 responses from each street combined into the one map. It becomes immediately obvious that as traffic volumes increased, the space people considered to be their home territory shrank.

The results from these two sections of his surveys are totally interrelated. People on Heavy street had less friends and acquaintances precisely because there was less home territory (exchange space) in which to interact socially. As one person from Medium street said about the increasing traffic, 'It used to be friendly; what was outside has now withdrawn into the buildings...'.[11]

Appleyard commented on his findings:

> There was a marked difference in the way these three streets were seen and used, especially by the young and the elderly.

> Light street was a closely knit community whose residents made full use of their street. The street had been divided into different use zones by the residents. Front steps were used for sitting and chatting, sidewalks for children playing, and for adults to stand and pass the time of day, especially around the corner store, and the roadway by children and teenagers for more active games like football. However the street was seen as a whole and no part was out of bounds. Heavy street, on the other hand, had little or no sidewalk activity and was used solely as a corridor between the sanctuary of individual homes and the outside world. Residents kept very much to themselves. There was no feeling of community at all. Medium street again seemed to fall somewhere between the two extremes. It was still quite an active social street, although there was no strong feeling of community and most activity was confined to the sidewalks where a finely sensed boundary separated pedestrians from traffic.[12]

Appleyard concluded his study:

> The contrast between the two streets [Heavy and Light] was striking. On the one hand alienation, on the other friendliness and involvement.[13]

This increase in zone-of-influence and shrinking of home territory is insidious and goes through distinctive stages (fig. 6). First to be subjugated is the actual carriageway. In Appleyard's account above it can be seen that on Light street the people still considered the carriageway to be part of their home territory. It was still a place for children to play and where people gathered to talk. But in Medium street, residents had lost control of the carriageway and felt confined to the footpath.

This subjugation of the carriageway involves a transfer of ownership. The traditional users (children and residents) lose ownership and the motorist takes ownership. Thus motorists view pedestrians, cyclists or children playing in the street as intruding into their space. Studies by Professor Stina Sandels show that as the speed of traffic increases, the attitude of motorists to pedestrians becomes increasingly ruthless.[14] Wide stretches of bitumen and fast flowing lanes of traffic reinforce drivers' perceptions that the street is their territory. An actual transfer of control or ownership takes place and this results in a shrinkage of people's home territory. Whether this transference of ownership is right or wrong will be examined later.

The next piece of the home territory to go is the footpath itself. As Appleyard observed, on Heavy street there was 'little or no sidewalk activity and [the sidewalk] was used solely as a corridor between the sanctuary of individual homes and the outside world'. This loss of ownership is in part due to the noise, dirt and vibration caused by the traffic. But it is also a result of the disappearance of people. When the children no longer play in the street and people drive instead of walk, then even the footpath becomes a barren no-man's land and the street loses its main attraction – people.

However, this shrinking of home territory does not stop at the front fence. Appleyard observed a dramatic drop-off in gardening or people simply sitting on their front steps on Heavy street. Thus traffic eventually claims even the front yard. But the takeover does not stop at the front door of the house. As one respondent from Heavy street said to Appleyard when asked to indicate his home territory; 'Just this apartment...not even that'. As traffic increases in their street numerous people are forced to abandon the front rooms of their homes because of the noise. Part, or in some cases the whole, of their home was lost as home territory.

The last step in this saga of shrinking home territory is that people abandon their homes completely and become traffic refugees. Appleyard observed that on Heavy street there were far fewer children than on Light street. 'The lack of children,' according to Appleyard, 'partly explained the impoverished social life on Heavy street; in fact many treated the street more as a transient hotel than as a residence'.[15] Those families who could, had fled. On Medium street these processes were also at work. As the traffic slowly increased, families were in the course of leaving. Those who remained expressed deep regrets at the demise of their street community.

It may be argued that those who replaced the families who fled are the kind of people who do not mind traffic noise and who do not want neighbourly relationships with others in their street. This ignores the plight of the families who at one time enjoyed a strong neighbourhood community and have now been forced to flee. For them, long-term meaningful relationships have been fractured.

It also ignores the plight of those who are unable to flee the threat; those who are elderly, disabled or those who simply cannot afford to relocate. As Appleyard says, 'These "trapped" residents may suffer more than any others'.[16] They must suffer not only the loss of lifelong friendships as friends flee, but also the ongoing intrusion of traffic into

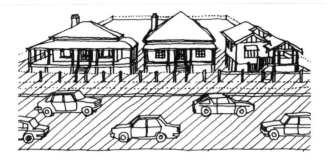

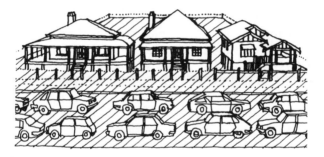

Fig. 6: The spreading zone-of-influence. As volume and speed of traffic increase, home territory is progressively eroded.

53

their living rooms. Worst of all, they are condemned to a permanent poverty of relationships because there is absolutely no hope of resurrecting or re-creating the sense of community they once enjoyed.

The argument that the kind of people who move in are not bothered by noise and not interested in relationships also ignores one other factor: these people may discover a rich dimension of life they never knew existed if they were to become part of a vibrant, caring neighbourhood. Perhaps they are being robbed of something they do not even know they need. However, I suspect the real reason these people locate on heavy traffic streets is more to do with economic imperatives than desire or lack of desire for neighbourhood life. They simply cannot afford to buy or rent elsewhere. For these people a lack of neighbourhood friendship links is just one more cost they must pay for their poor economic situation.

This take-over of home territory (the primary space for spontaneous exchange) by traffic cannot be measured simply by looking at how much of a city has been transformed to road space. Subjugation is a subtle process unrecognised by most city planners. It was this process that provoked a resident to tell a consultant, 'I don't care what your predictions for future traffic growth are. Just give us back some of the quality of life we enjoyed 15 years ago'.

Appleyard's research is backed by much anecdotal evidence, such as the elderly lady I met on my first doorknock along Route 20. She had not ventured outside her front door for three months and I had to yell at her through the security door, not because she was deaf, but because of the noise coming from the road outside. For this lady, times had changed. The world outside her front door had become so hostile, she no longer felt safe outside the walls of her home. She felt her house was under siege from traffic.

A man told how once he and his wife had a number of friends on the other side of their street. A couple of years previously their street was widened to four lanes and immediately there was a dramatic increase in traffic. Because of the increase in traffic, he and his wife no longer felt safe crossing the road and had stopped visiting their friends. The friendships had died.

Another resident told how the neighbours in his street, in times past, had regularly gathered together for a street barbecue. As the traffic increased, these street activities decreased. But a strange thing happened. Large roadworks at the entrance to their street resulted in a dramatic drop in traffic on their street for a period of about six months. The result? A resurrection of many of the old neighbourhood links and an increase of children playing in the street.

As home territory shrinks so does the opportunity for social interaction and spontaneous exchange. Hostile territory is not the place where people hold intimate conversations. Chuck Berry's prophetic words express, in another way, the results of the increasing zone-of-influence with its erosion of home territory and spontaneous exchange: loss of place.

> Riding along in my automobile,
> My baby beside me at the wheel,
> Cruising and playing the radio,
> And no particular place to go.

Burning the house to stay warm

Earlier I discussed how the introduction of the cane toads upset the delicate web of relationships. What I have been suggesting since is that the introduction of the car into the Eco-City unsettles a range of relationships and sets up chain reactions that feed on themselves. Cars compete for space and converting exchange space to movement space spreads the city which demands more travel which demands more space. Similarly, car traffic erodes home territory and the opportunity for spontaneous exchange. To make up for these lost exchanges, additional trips must be made which in turn further erodes home territory and spontaneous exchange.

As well, increased road infrastructure encourages inefficiencies such as cross-commuting, which puts more traffic on the roads, which demands bigger roads which encourages further inefficiencies. But the domination of the car also sets up numerous other feedback loops.

Increase in trip frequencies
New and upgraded roads encourage people to increase the frequency of trips. Instead of visiting Aunt Meg once a fortnight they now visit once a week. Again this seems like a benefit until we realise two things. Firstly, in a more compact city (a city which has turned over less of its living space to road space) Aunt Meg may be living just around the corner or within walking distance. Secondly, the illusion of greater accessibility to Aunt Meg may not only encourage an increase in frequency of visits; it may also encourage a decrease in the length of visits. In the old days it may have taken three hours travelling by horse and cart to visit Aunt Meg. But visitors stayed the whole day. Today people spend 45 minutes travelling, but only stay for 30 minutes. In other words, greater road infrastructure promotes a pattern of living which actually increases the time spent travelling as opposed to enjoying the reason for which the trip was made.

Decreased viability of public transport

The more spread-out a city becomes, the less viable its public transport. Instead of the bus travelling one kilometre to pick up ten passengers, it has to drive ten kilometres. Rail, light rail and underground rail are even more uneconomical in a spread out city because of the very high capital costs of providing the tracks in the first place. New roads also lure customers away from public transport, further eroding its viability. As the public transport system runs down, more people are forced to switch to private cars to maintain their previous levels of access to exchange opportunities.

Moving of destinations outside walk and cycle range

As the city spreads an increasing number of destinations are moved outside of the cycle and walking range. Once a person switches to a private car for these trips, they then lose a range of spontaneous exchange opportunities which must be compensated for by more trips.

Erosion of walk and cycle space

In some cases footpaths are narrowed or disappear completely. In other cases the footpath 'feels' unsafe because of the proximity and speed of the traffic. One of the little understood effects of this is on the use of public transport. Almost every public transport trip starts with a walk or cycle journey. If it is too dangerous to cross a road to a bus stop, people, if they have the option, will often opt to drive their car.

Erosion of more benign means of transport is a good example of how these feedback cycles work. For example, many parents drive their children to school because it is too dangerous for them to walk or cycle; hence, they add to the very problem they are trying to overcome. In turn, other parents are then forced to drive their children.

Death of the corner store

The reasons why increasing road infrastructure kills off the neighbour-hood store and local shopping centre are many:

- Neighbourhood stores are usually on the busiest roads and therefore are often the first victims of road widening.

- The building of wide roads to large regional shopping complexes has encouraged people to shop at national/multinational chains thus eroding the viability of neighbourhood stores.

- As traffic increases in front of the store, the store comes into the zone-of-influence and thus becomes hostile territory, losing its charm as socialising space.

- The conversion of homes to road space means a decrease in the number of patrons for the store, thereby eroding its viability. As a store closes or becomes unviable, local employment decreases which further decreases the number of customers working and living in the area, making other stores less viable. The dominoes fall one by one.

Death of the neighbourhood store makes a surprising contribution to a reduction in social contact. It is not just the contact with the store owner, a valuable social contact in its own right, which is lost. Casual contacts which occur spontaneously on the way to the store are also lost. The end result is people are removed from the streets, further adding to the sense that the streets have been abandoned and handed over to traffic and no longer belong to the neighbourhood.

I remember standing and studying the community life of a traffic calmed street corner in Cologne. The street had been modified to slow traffic to walking speed and the intersection had been significantly narrowed. On the corner was a neighbourhood store, some houses, a post with a brass sculptured hat and some interesting wrought-iron work for people to park their bikes against. The intersection was paved and landscaped. You could feel the neighbourliness just by standing and watching. A four year old girl arrived on a tricycle, riding on the roadway, with her grandfather walking beside her. They stopped and talked for 20 minutes to the shopkeeper. I could not help wondering what would have happened to this level of community interaction if, instead of narrowing the roadway, authorities had followed the Los Angeles pattern by pulling the shop down and widening the intersection.

The death of the corner store is one of the factors in what sociologists call 'urban blight', a cancer that slowly eats its way through an entire neighbourhood.

Fear of crime
It is fairly well accepted that people who feel alienated from their society are more likely to take out their frustrations on society by some violent act. But what is not equally recognised is that one of the major causes of that alienation, loss of the road and pavement as exchange space, also increases the opportunity for crime.

One of the greatest deterrents to would-be criminals are curious eyes. Rapists and muggers usually choose dark parks, car parks or deserted streets as the scene of their attacks, far from prying eyes. Vibrant neighbourhoods, where the streets are alive with people and people are watching the street-life from their gardens and windows, are places which are inherently safer than deserted streets where curtains are drawn. Here, again, it is easy to see how these feedback cycles feed on themselves. Once there have been one or two muggings, thefts, or rapes in these deserted streets, fear begins to rule, further diminishing the attractiveness of the street for people and thus making it more unsafe.

One reaction when fear rules the streets is to take refuge in vehicles. As Jane Jacobs says, 'This is the technique practised in the big wild-animal reservations in Africa, where tourists are warned to leave their cars under no circumstances until they reach a lodge. It is also the technique practised in Los Angeles'.[17] With a rate for rape twice that of any other city, is it any wonder that the people of Los Angeles feel they must take refuge in their cars? In Donald Appleyard's study, the fear of crime was almost three times higher on Heavy street as on Light street. People had not abandoned the street just because of the traffic.

There is an incredible sense of fear that settles on Los Angeles as soon as it is dark. At night I felt totally afraid even though the wail of police sirens could be heard and police cars seemed to be everywhere. If anyone came within fifty metres I would start running.

The contrast with the friendliness and sense of community in most European cities was striking. For example, I arrived in Hamburg at night and asked a man if he could show me on a map where I was. He did not speak English, but a woman walking past overheard and asked if she could help. She spoke only broken English and I asked if she could point out where I was. Instead, she asked where I wanted to go. I explained I wanted to walk to the Youth Hostel. She insisted on walking with me and showing me the way. One and a half hours later, well after 9.30 pm, she delivered me right to the door of the hostel. On the way she had taken me on a guided tour of the city explaining all the highlights. At no time did I feel afraid.

What Appleyard discovered in microcosm, I saw transferred to whole cities. In Los Angeles, the streets had been abandoned. Alienation ruled by day and fear by night. In cities where higher priority was placed on public transport, bikes and walking, the streets were alive with human activities and a sense of neighbourliness ruled. They could even leave their chairs in the city square!

As Bertrand Le Gendre wrote, 'Violence in towns is first of all the violence which has been done to the towns themselves. Theft is encouraged by the feeling that nothing belongs to anyone, at least not to anyone who can be identified'.[18]

Atomisation of society

There is an ironic twist to this whole scenario of traffic eroding the level of social interaction in a community. More and more demand is placed on the individual members of a family to meet each other's entire range of social, emotional and spiritual needs. Many relationships cannot stand this unnatural demand and crack under the strain, in some cases fracturing the most important of all human relationships. While I would not go so far as to blame the automobile for the incredible increase in family breakdown, it is nonetheless a very important element in understanding the atomisation of society and the resultant plague of alienation.

The feedback cycle, in this case, is that as the basic unit of society has shrunk from the tribe to the one- or two-person family, increasing demand has been placed on support systems outside the home or neighbourhood to meet those needs that were once met internally.

The Nuremburg experience

I related earlier how my experience of the main street of Nuremburg led me to an understanding of the concept of spontaneous exchange. As I reflected on this idea a fairly radical concept began to form. I asked myself how the people of Nuremburg would replace the wide range of spontaneous exchange opportunities being enjoyed in the street, if the 30,000 vehicles were allowed back into the street again. It suddenly dawned on me that it was possible to travel more yet end up with less exchange.

This was the idea I began developing for the 1991 International Transport Conference. I showed an early draft of my paper to Bill Croft, a lateral-thinking engineer who was heading up a passenger transport review for South-East Queensland. He was excited by the possibilities but told me that if engineers were to grasp the concept they would need some graphs. On the white board in his office he drew the graph shown in fig. 7. It was a stroke of genius because it helps explain the concept that while movement (travel) is necessary to facilitate some exchange, it simultaneously erodes exchange. There are four stages to this process.

- **Stage One: Rapid Growth in Exchange Opportunities**
  Initial provisions for travel produce a net increase in exchanges because traffic levels are not yet at a sufficient level to greatly diminish spontaneous exchange or demand that exchange space be converted to movement space.

- **Stage Two: Decreasing Rate of Return**
  As traffic increases it erodes greater amounts of spontaneous exchange and the city spreads as increasing amounts of space are dedicated to movement infrastructure. The feedback cycles outlined above result in decreasing rates of return. In other words, the travel is not as productive as it was in Stage One because the gains are being eroded by the feedback cycles. In Stage One, doubling movement doubled exchange opportunities. In Stage Two, doubling movement may only give 30 per cent increase in exchange opportunities.

- **Stage Three: Equilibrium**
  In Stage Three equilibrium is reached. In other words, any further gains in exchange are cancelled by the losses incurred because of the numerous feedback loops discussed earlier.

- **Stage Four: Getting Less for More**
  In Stage Four the feedback cycles set up by any attempt to increase movement are not only self-cancelling (Stage Three) but begin to eat into the previous gains in exchange opportunities; in other words, getting less exchange for more travel. Unfortunately this is the stage which our car-dominated cities have reached. This is the stage where people destroy their destinations in going to them. It is a bit like breaking up your house and burning it in the fireplace to stay warm. Eventually you are left out in the cold with no house and no fire.

The logical conclusion from understanding this process is that cities that have entered Stage Three or Four could offer their citizens higher levels of exchange for less travelling by reducing road infrastructure and turning it back into exchange space.

Some people will protest that surely people have access to a wider range of facilities opened up by the car. This is true taking a short-term view. If I was a pedestrian yesterday and a motorist today, then there is no argument that I have greater mobility today than I had yesterday. But what is being explored here are not the short-term consequences of one person's choice, but the medium to long-term consequences of collective choices. Talk to those who remember the city before the car took over,

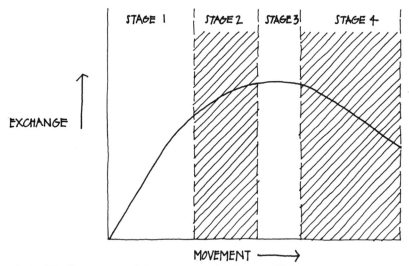

Fig. 7: The four stages of the movement/exchange efficiency curve.

or visit Los Angeles and then Nuremburg and it will be seen that the Exchange Efficiency Curve is no fantasy. We *are* going backwards.

Getting more with less

Some forms of transport are more 'exchange friendly' than others. In other words, some forms of transport are more savage in their erosion of spontaneous exchange and have a more ferocious appetite for space; they therefore produce stronger feedback effects. Walking, cycling and public transport facilitate spontaneous exchange rather than destroy it and are more space-efficient than cars, so it is possible to increase movement without making the same demands for exchange space to be converted to movement space. Nor do they contribute to the cycles of fear of crime like cars. Thus cities which rely on exchange-friendly forms of transport will have much higher returns of exchange opportunities for the same amount of movement because the feedback effects do not undermine the gains to the same extent (fig. 8).

A nudge is as good as a wink

In *Chaos – Making a New Science*, James Gleick tells how Edward Lorenz, in 1961, stumbled upon a discovery that was the beginning of a whole new science.[19] As a child Lorenz was fascinated by mathematical puzzles and after graduating from Dartmouth College in 1938 he was convinced that mathematics was his calling. But World War II intervened and he found himself in the Army Air Corps working as a weather forecaster.

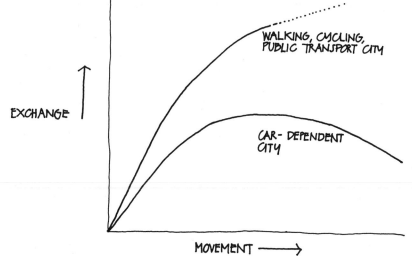

Fig. 8: Exchange-friendly transport gives a higher yield of exchange.

After the war he decided to combine his two interests and apply his mathematics to meteorology. Along with all Western scientists, Lorenz believed in the Newtonian promise of a deterministic world in which one could tell with absolute surety how the world would unfold, providing you understood the rules.

Lorenz also accepted another fundamental tenet of Western science which one theoretician put as follows:

> The basic idea of Western science is that you don't have to take into account the falling of a leaf on some planet in another galaxy when you're trying to account for the motion of a billiard ball on a pool table on earth. Very small influences can be neglected. There's a convergence in the way things work, and arbitrarily small influences do not blow up to have arbitrarily large effects.[20]

What concerned Lorenz was the big weather picture. Surely global weather patterns could be predicted if one had the time to do the myriad of calculations needed? In 1960 Lorenz obtained the means in the form of a noisy, bulky Royal McBee computer. Lorenz decided to build a simplified version of world weather patterns using just 12 of the variables that affected weather. It was a toy world. Gleick takes up the story:

> He was the god of this machine universe, free to choose the laws of nature as he pleased. After a certain amount of undivine trial and error, he chose 12. They were numerical rules – equations that expressed the relationships between temperature and pressure, between pressure and wind speed. Lorenz understood that he was putting into practice the laws of Newton, appropriate tools of a clockmaker deity who could create a world and set it running for eternity.[21]

Lorenz's toy weather world fascinated his colleagues. Punch in a set of 12 conditions and every minute the computer would print out a list of figures that for the initiated told the story of the weather for that day; winds shifting from north to south, digitised cyclones whirling across the page. Colleagues and graduate students would gather round and lay bets on what Lorenz's toy weather world would do next.

Lorenz created a primitive way of printing out graphs for each of the 12 variables. One day in the winter of 1961 he decided to examine one of these graph sequences in greater detail. Instead of re-running the whole program from the beginning he decided to start in the middle by typing in the appropriate figures for the 12 conditions as indicated on a printout for the day at which he wanted to start. Setting the computer going he went down the hall to make a cup of coffee and get away from the noisy machine. When he returned something had gone drastically wrong.

The forecasted weather should have been the same for both computer runs. Exactly the same preconditions had been entered and he had not changed the rules of his toy universe. But as Lorenz stared at the new printout the weather bore no resemblance to what had been predicted in the computer run the day before. In fact, for some days the predictions were exact opposites. He was bewildered. What could have gone wrong? Was it a faulty vacuum tube? Suddenly the reason dawned. His computer made calculations to six decimal points. But his printout was only to three decimal points. So while the computer had stored 0.506127 it had printed out 0.506.

But why should this make such a huge difference? It represented a change of just one part in ten thousand. It was almost impossible for meteorologists even to measure this much difference in, say, the temperature of the ocean. Lorenz had assumed that given a certain starting point the weather would always unfold the same way. If you changed the starting point slightly, the outcome would change slightly. His one part in a thousand error was like a small puff of wind. Surely these small puffs of wind just dissipated or were cancelled by some other one-part-in-a-thousand puff of wind? Yet Lorenz's computer had just told him that a small puff of wind could change the weather pattern over the whole globe within two months.

In the next few days Lorenz set out to confirm his accidental finding that small changes could produce catastrophic changes. Changing just one small input he would overlay the results. Always it was the same, wide divergence in a very short time. For Lorenz, long range forecasting was doomed. What Lorenz discovered became known as the Butterfly Effect: a butterfly's wing flap in China may be the cause of a hurricane in Florida a week later.

Planners are only beginning to ask what the implications of chaos may be for their traffic and population long range computer forecasting. Could knocking down one corner store to widen an intersection be the flap of a butterfly's wing that puts the whole city's transport into chaos? One of the few who have seen the link and started applying the insights of chaos to city planning is T. Cartwright. He says:

> Gathering more information or constructing more elaborate models about chaotic systems can become pointless. In fact 'research' can even be counter-productive, if it creates a false sense of security about planning and what it can do. Our ability to predict the behaviour of chaotic systems is inherently limited... Looking for more accurate models of housing demand or traffic flow [is] potentially a fool's errand if these phenomena are indeed chaotic.[22]

Cartwright is feeling his way. He is not sure whether the city is a chaotic system or not; or when it may become chaotic. He confuses himself because he begins by examining how chaos arises in a system with two variables that interact; in his study, a population which grows at a fixed rate (births over natural death) and the limitations imposed by the environment on total population (overcrowding, disease, food shortages, losses to predators, etc.). By applying simple mathematical formulae, Cartwright found what chaos scientists have found for all two element systems (for example a flame heating a pot of water); the system goes through three distinct stages depending on the initial settings of the two variables. These stages are: stable equilibrium – either extinction or a stable population; dynamic equilibrium – predictable cycles of boom and bust; and chaos – unpredictable but with 'islands' of order.

But like the weather, the city is not a two element or even a 12 element system. There are a myriad of variables that influence traffic and population levels. By far the most important consideration, and the one that automatically makes both the weather and cities chaotic, is the element of self-determination. The butterfly has the power of choice, and exercise of its free will to flap its wings at a crucial moment in a crucial place may change the entire weather of the planet in just two months. Similarly, one person deciding to knock down one shop to widen one intersection may change the city's entire traffic system within a very short time; I suspect as little as two to five years.

It seems impossible until you see how it works in reality. For example, the council recently decided to widen the road through our local shopping centre. When I complained to the person responsible for the decision I was told it was only a minor piece of work that would have no impact. I explained that it would dispossess ten local businesses. He replied that he had surveyed the area and found there were enough vacant shops for them all to relocate locally. I told him this was naive in the extreme. I continued:

> The vacant shops are all in a new, up-market development where rents are three to ten times higher. Surely you understand that a shopping centre needs a mix of old and new shops? Businesses that are marginal need the older shops where rents are lower. Force these into a high rent situation and in six to 12 months they will be out of business. This will immediately affect the viability of all the other shop owners. For example, one of the shops is a specialist bed shop. There are no other premises big enough so the owners intend closing permanently. At the moment this shop attracts people in the market for a bed from the whole region, and while in Ashgrove these people may buy a pie, a drink, get their hair cut, or lay-by a dress. Those people won't come now. In the end other businesses will become marginal and close down, taking others with them.

> When the shopping centre eventually runs down, people will be forced to drive to a regional shopping centre. This new traffic will demand that roads through other shopping centres be widened and so the cancerous process will start all over again in someone else's neighbourhood. Minor works indeed, but city-wide implications.

This is the process of urban blight; the creation of one cancerous cell that infects others and destroys an entire neighbourhood and eventually an entire city.

The late Father Graham Perry told the following story in CART's very first community newspaper:

> When I first came to live in Brisbane, I obtained an apprenticeship in Annerley. After a great deal of searching I found accommodation in an old boarding house. Nothing fancy, but comfortable. But my stay was short-lived because the City Council wanted to widen Ipswich Road to take more traffic. So I moved to another place behind the tram depot opposite the PA Hospital. It was a relatively quiet, friendly community. People cared for each other and were proud of their area. I attended the Thompson Estate Anglican Church which was packed with friendly people. This church typified the many other vibrant community groups in the district. But all this changed. The tranquil suburb of Annerley has been shattered by the South Eastern Freeway, soaring thirty feet above the rooftops. Going back to the suburb you now find a split community... Empty shops... Empty churches. A suburb without soul.[23]

Marshall Berman calls this process of urban blight 'urbicide: murder of a city'. In a stirring article in the *New Internationalist*, Berman described how urban blight destroyed the once proud neighbourhood of his childhood in New York.

> The South Bronx, where I spent my childhood and youth, is the site of one of the greatest recent ruins today outside Beirut. The physical and social destruction of the area began with the construction of the Cross Bronx Expressway in the late 1950s and early 1960s spreading gradually southward from the highway and northward from the emerging Bruckner Expressway in the late sixties.

> Then in the early 1970s the disintegration began to spread at a spectacular pace, devouring house after house and block after block, displacing thousands of people like some inexorable plague. Those were the years when the Bronx finally made it into the media, as a symbol of every disaster that could happen to a city. 'The Bronx Is Burning!' resonated all over the world...

> Every time I saw or heard about another landmark (streets I'd played in, houses where friends lived; schools, shops, synagogues) I felt a piece of my flesh was being ripped away...

> In our sense of loss and violation we have plenty of company. In the South Bronx alone, more than 30,000 people fled in the 1970s as their homes were being destroyed. Many of these people were forced to run more than once, trying to stay ahead of the blight that kept catching up with them. Thousands more in Manhattan and in Brooklyn went through the same ordeal. In fact something similar was happening in working-class neighbourhoods in older cities all over the US...[24]

While both these examples are dramatic in that they are not the gentle nudge of a butterfly's wings but the mad hacking of a meat axe, they nevertheless concentrate into a snapshot the possible long-term effects of the gentle nudge (or wink to a developer or road builder).

But while the science of chaos may be frightening with the long-term implications of a nudge or a wink, it also holds incredible promise. The solutions to our traffic problems may not demand the draconian, sledgehammer measures we fear. If a nudge and a wink is enough to lead us into a mess, a nudge and a wink may be all that is needed to pull us out. The future art of city building is knowing the critical time and the critical place to flutter the wings.

3   Eco-relational thinking

The theatre was revolutionized by the Stanislavski acting method, which evolved from the concept that the true understanding necessary for great contemporary acting must come from the actor's internal understanding of the situation, not from the mimicry of external physical expressions. The environmental design profession awaits a similiar revolution...
Laurence Stephan Cutler &
Sherrie Stephens-Cutler[1]

I will return to Jerusalem, my holy city, and live there. It will be known as the faithful city... Once again old men and women, so old that they use a stick when they walk, will be sitting in the city squares. And the streets will again be full of boys and girls playing.
Zechariah, 520BC[2]

More power to the generalist

A couple of days after the formation of the CART committee I door-knocked for six hours looking for someone who would be prepared to speak to a reporter about their plight. Without exception I received the same response from every resident: 'Once the government makes up its mind to do something there is nothing you can do to stop it'. At the first committee meeting I enthused about how we were going to win; but I was alone in my enthusiasm. 'You can't beat them', I was counselled, 'but we'll give them a hell of a fight'.

These responses are indicative of an overwhelming feeling of loss of control throughout the whole of society which has frightening implications. The statements by both the residents and the committee sound more like those you would expect to hear in a totalitarian state. They eat away at the very foundations of a democratic society where people are supposed to govern their own affairs and community life through elected representatives.

In a democracy, elected representatives and their helpers are called 'public servants'. These servants are employed by the community to steer the corporate ship. The community, as those being served, are meant to decide where they want the ship to go. So what has gone wrong when whole communities think that the ship is heading for the rocks yet feel powerless to change its direction? We may be tempted to think the servants have mutinied and hijacked the ship. But the truth is more likely that the community has become a victim of its own self-doubt. Self-doubt bred by our society's move to specialisation.

Until the Industrial Revolution, society, by and large, had an agricultural base and people were *generalists*. They built their own homes, made their own clothes, built their own furniture, doctored their own animals, farmed their own land, and provided their own entertainment. In general, these people had an incredible faith in their own ability to tackle any task and make a good fist of it. They had a quiet confidence, built up through practical experience, that they could adapt to any task. They also had an inbred streak of ingenuity. When faced with a problem and a lack of resources, they could think laterally and devise creative solutions.

In modern society all that has changed. We have become a society of *specialists*. We have carpenters to build our homes. Plumbers to do the plumbing. Seamstresses to make our clothes. Cabinet makers to make our furniture. Veterinarians to doctor our animals. Agriculturalists to grow our food. Entertainers to entertain us. Town planners to plan our cities. Engineers to design our roads. And in each of these fields we have 'experts'.

This trend to specialisation has first of all led to a dramatic decline in people's faith in their own ability to tackle a variety of tasks and succeed. That confidence can only come through the practical experience of tackling a wide range of tasks and succeeding. In today's society many people only ever conquer one specialised area and even then there is much self-doubt because there is always someone who is even more of an expert!

The second result has been the death of innovation – creative ingenuity in problem solving. A recent study carried out in the US found that 80 per cent of six year-olds were creative but only 10 per cent of 40 year-olds.[3] Somewhere between the ages of six and 40 our society kills off creativity.

One of the major reasons is that when faced with a problem, we call for an expert. But the expert is often not required to dig in the deep recesses of their imagination to find a creative solution either. They merely must know which text book to consult. If they need to think creatively it is within a certain artificially defined mono-knowledge field. Thus, the structural engineer may exert some creative powers in designing a bridge to span a river to allow people access to a range of exchange opportunities, but is not encouraged to think creatively about whether the bridge is the best solution to the problem of maximising exchange while minimising travel. Maybe, instead of building a bridge to take people to the facilities, the facilities could be bought to the people.

This crisis of confidence and loss of creativity in our society has had a number of important consequences:

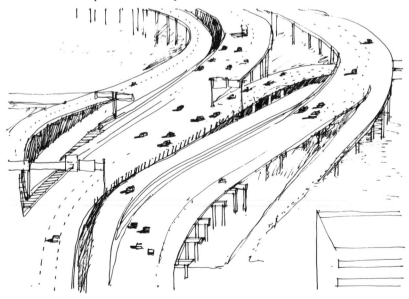

■ Because of the enormous complexity of the world today, people leave decision-making to 'experts'.

■ When things are seen to be out of control, for example the growth and dominance of traffic in the city, people feel powerless to exert their authority.

■ The fragmentation of knowledge means many decisions are made without looking at 'the big picture'. The traffic engineer's job is to design roads to provide for future demands, not to ask whether this will lead to an efficient or inefficient city. That is the job of a town planner. It is not the traffic engineer's job to ask whether building bigger roads is destroying the social fabric of our cities. That is the job of a social planner.

■ Even more disturbing is the divorce of decision-making from its moral and ethical implications. The structural engineer is presented with a specific problem; please build a flyover between points A and B capable of carrying Y quantity of traffic. The engineer is not asked first to consider who will benefit and who will be harmed by such a proposal. There is no consideration given, for instance, to whether the flyover will give greater access to exchange opportunities to a wealthy section of the community at the expense of a poorer section.

■ Experts become defensive about their area of specialisation. In most cases a great portion of the expert's self-identity and self-esteem resides in the area of expertise. Any suggestion that there are different solutions, or that the expert is not seeing the big picture, or that current solutions are not working, is seen as a personal attack.

■ Solutions are being proposed which are no longer appropriate. Because the expert does not have to think creatively about solutions or even the nature of a problem but simply needs to know which text book to use, solutions tend to become institutionalised. To propose a different solution is to swim against the tide and risk the derision of peers. But because the world is ever-changing these institutionalised solutions may no longer work. In fact, the solutions of yesterday are often the problems of today.

From what I have said so far it may appear that I am against the expert and the move to specialisation. This is not the case since everyone benefits from having experts in society. What I am arguing against is experts as those being served rather than serving the people. As servants, experts may provide specialised knowledge about one particular part of a problem and thus help communities to find innovative solutions.

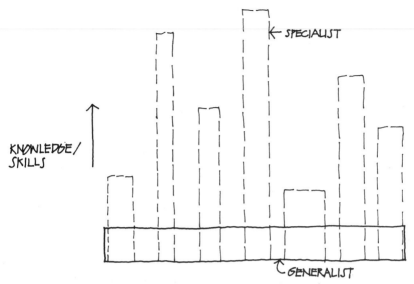

Fig. 9: The knowledge/skills map for generalists and specialists.

Society needs, once again, to recognise the role of the generalist. While specialists have narrow, vertical fields of knowledge which are usually separated from other narrow vertical fields, the generalist is an eco-relational thinker who tries to integrate and see the relationships between these separated fields. On the map of knowledge/skills (see fig. 9) the generalist has a horizontal field which spans a small portion of each of the specialist fields. This spanning of the specialist areas allows the generalist to reach up and call down the knowledge needed to understand an issue and design new creative solutions. The expert is therefore the servant of the generalist.

Another way of viewing the generalist is to see a person who does not fence off areas of knowledge into artificially determined paddocks. It reminds me of the story of the duck farmers on a river plain who kept their ducks fenced in, until the floods came when the fences became submerged and the ducks swam together. The generalist submerges the fences and allows the ducks who have been kept separate to swim together. Whilst this creates 'chaos', it does allow the ducks to associate together and cross breed.

It is possible for a specialist also to be a generalist. Every field of specialisation has those lateral thinkers who challenge accepted wisdom. But what these people are doing is interpreting their field of specialisation in the light of their generalist knowledge, not interpreting their life experience in the light of their specialisation. They own some ducks but they are more than happy to let them swim with everyone else's.

About 12 months ago I presented a paper on the subject of generalists and specialists to a university audience. One of the lecturers stood up at the end and commented that what frightened him was that every one of his students entered the institution as a generalist. They brought with them a vast array of life experience. But somehow in the educational process they jettisoned this body of knowledge and became specialists in which their specialisation was divorced entirely from their life experience.

Experience tells us that non-specialists have a knack of observing real life and coming to sensible conclusions. One day I was chatting to a shop keeper about a very dangerous pedestrian crossing in a shopping centre where a child had been knocked down the day before. He said that when the council was installing the crossing he had told them it would be dangerous. The crossing was located about 50 metres from an intersection controlled by traffic lights. The proprietor had explained to these planning 'experts' that as motorists approached the intersection, they would be more interested in speeding up to catch the green light than looking sideways to see if someone was about to step off the footpath onto the crossing. His home-grown wisdom was ignored and people have been needlessly injured ever since.

This man was bringing his life experience to bear on a particular 'technical' situation. How did he know people speed up as they approach a green light? He probably had done it himself a thousand times. He simply became aware of a relationship which forms itself when you mix a motorist, a powerful car and a green light. If the specialist engineers had brought their life experience to the problem of this crossing they probably would have reached the same conclusions.

Jane Jacobs tells the story of how she became addicted to the public hearings of the New York Board of Estimates:

> ...the proceedings are heartening because of the abounding vitality, earnestness and sense with which so many citizens rise to the occasion. Very plain people, including the poor, including the discriminated against, including the uneducated, reveal themselves momentarily as people with grains of greatness in them, and I do not speak sardonically. They tell with wisdom and often eloquence about things they know first hand from life. They speak with passion about concerns that are local but far from narrow.[4]

Residents along busy roads are always far greater experts than the so-called experts. Elderly people do not need expensive noise-measuring equipment to know when noise levels are too high. They simply listen. Children do not need degrees and expensive analysing equipment to know when air pollution has reached unacceptable levels. They simply breathe. Residents who know nothing about V/C ratios can tell when there is too much traffic on a road. They simply try to cross it to visit a friend.

This contention that residents are the real 'experts' is not some oversimplification. It is a recognition of why we have cities in the first place. The fundamental reason we establish cities is to enhance the quality of life of people. Unless this happens there is no point in continuing with them.

Cities are not just units of economic production. Nor are they institutions for the paternalistic custodial care of the unwashed masses who must be kept under control for their own good. Cities are for people; or to be more correct, cities are people; or to be even more precise, cities are a concentration of people interrelating. The city is a family which inhabits a house and, by its presence, the family makes the house a home. That family modifies the house as time proceeds to enhance their quality of life and the quality of their relationships to each other. People may employ architects to help them, but it is their needs as human beings they are seeking to satisfy. So it is in a neighbourhood and a city.

This contention that residents are the real experts is also a recognition that ultimate reality is not the material universe but our experience of it. It is interesting that in the examples I gave earlier to back up my claim that ordinary people are the experts, experience of real life was the source of insight. The man's insight into the behaviour of motorists faced with a green light either came from reflecting on his own reaction to green lights, or by being nearly knocked over by a motorist speeding up to 'catch' a green light. It came from an understanding of human nature; the impetuous drive to save time. What struck Jane Jacobs at the Board of Estimates hearings was that people told about things they knew first hand from life with wisdom and eloquence.

What society needs to recover is the concept that every person is already a generalist. The surgeon who specialises in heart and lung transplants and the kindergarten teacher have one thing in common: when it comes to traffic, or any other thing that affects the vitality of their neighbourhood, they are both generalists. And as generalists they are in a much better position to make decisions about the level of roadspace to be provided in their neighbourhood than the traffic engineers – unless the engineers are willing to submit their profession to their own and other people's life experience.

While I have concentrated on the move to specialisation as one of the reasons for the death of creativity in society, the suffocating sense of powerlessness itself kills off creativity. As Saul Alinsky wrote, 'If people feel they don't have the power to change a bad situation, then they don't think about it. Why start figuring out how you are going to spend a million dollars if you do not have a million dollars...'.[5]

It is therefore imperative that a re-empowering process contain two distinct strands: encouraging people to believe in their ability to think and make decisions as generalists; and new structures that will facilitate genuine participation in the decision-making process. Part of this process will be a new emphasis in our universities which have become too specialised. It will involve teaching students the gentle art of eco-relational thinking – stressing that their specialist knowledge must always be subservient to their generalist knowledge.

Elevating the role of the generalist in our cities will eventually change not only the physical structure of our cities, but also the administrative and political structures, for they too are part of the intricate web of relationships that make up the Eco-City.

Learning the gentle art

The chief mental process for the generalist should be eco-relational thinking. When I mentioned to a friend that I had coined this term, he accused me of using a tautology. The prefix eco is an abbreviation of the word ecology which means the study of the relationships between organisms and their environment. I argued that, while he was technically correct, in common with most other things in life even the study of eco-systems has fallen into the domain of mechanistic thinking with the eco-system being separated out into its machine parts. I wanted to put back a meaning that had to some extent been lost.

From all that has been said so far, some people may gain the impression that there is no place for mechanistic modes of thought. But not so, because eco-relational thinking does not annihilate machine models, it subsumes them. The machine model is useful for understanding how some elements of an eco-system work, such as arms which act as levers and hearts that act as pumps. Such machine models are also useful for designing chairs that do not collapse when the people of Paris or Munich sit on them. But these machine models are useless in describing the *role* of these chairs in city life. They cannot predict the benefit of placing chairs in straight rows facing out as opposed to clustered around the table. Machine models are also useful for designing bridges that will carry traffic and not collapse. But these same models cannot describe the part this bridge will play in the intimate web of relationships in the Eco-City. They cannot tell whether the bridge is the best way of optimising exchange or facilitating greater participation by the easily marginalised in city life.

The problem of the past has been that we have tried to use mechanistic thought-forms (which work wonderfully with machines) when thinking about eco-systems. I shall explore for a moment the difference between machines and eco-systems and see what implications this has for the thinking process when dealing with eco-systems.

Stable and predictive versus dynamic and surprising

Machines have predictable, stable outputs. Change input A and, providing you know all the laws that govern the machine, the output is predictable. But in an eco-system the elements have self-determination which makes for a dynamic system that often surprises. Science is finding that even mechanical systems are impacted by the eco-system in which they find themselves. For example, a simple double pendulum is so sensitive to initial conditions that the gravitational pull of a single raindrop two kilometres away mixes up the motion within 50 to 60 revolutions, within about two minutes.[6]

Eco-relational thinking, therefore, accepts uncertainty and chaos, not only as part of the universe, but also as part of the thinking process. At the same time it looks for the spontaneous, the spark that comes when worlds collide. It waits expectantly for the new order that will arise, the nature of which will always be a surprise. It is not that there is no order in eco-systems. Order and beauty abound. I have already explored this order and beauty in the Paris street scene, in Nuremburg and in Munich. This is not the order and beauty of a machine which has no drive to evolve higher levels of order and beauty; this is the order and beauty of life which, through self-determination, turns chaos into new life forms and new levels of order.

Eco-relational thinking is therefore not always 'logical' in the traditional sense. It is often intuitive in that it connects the previously unconnected.

Linear versus circular

Machines are linear: A produces B. Eco-systems are cyclic: night and day; winter, spring, summer, autumn; life and death. Mechanistic thinking proceeds linearly towards deduction. Eco-relational thinking moves in circles. This not only applies to *what* we perceive, but *how* we perceive. In other words, eco-relational thinking not only looks for the cycles and feedback loops in the eco-system, it uses circular thinking patterns to understand these cycles. Thus an eco-relational thinker can start by looking at any one element of an event – for example the chairs in the Paris street – and from that one element gain a holistic understanding of the relationship between all elements. In this case a holistic understanding of the city as a place for exchange.

Alternatively, one can start with a holistic (macro level) understanding and by applying it to a specific event, be led back to an understanding

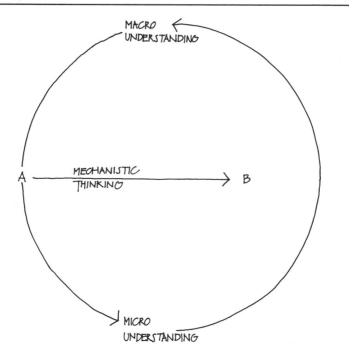

Fig. 10: The linear, mono-directional, mono-dimensional thought patterns of mechanistc thinking compared to eco-relational thinking which is circular.

of how the city works at the micro level. For example, by applying the lessons of exchange learnt from the Paris seats to the Nuremburg street, I was led back to an understanding of spontaneous exchange and its implications for diversity. The fascinating thing about this form of thinking is that you can go around and back around the circle from macro to micro, or micro to macro, and each time you go around your understanding is further enriched. Even in writing this book I was challenged to break out of my linear, hierarchical thinking patterns and to write 'in circles'. And so while the book is broken into sections, each with a major theme, I keep coming back to themes I encountered before, only each time I re-visit those themes it is with the insights I have gleaned from my previous trip round. Fig. 10 contrasts the linear thought forms of mechanistic thinking to circular thought forms of eco-relational thinking which constantly oscillates between a macro and micro understanding.

Mono-dimensional versus multi-dimensional
Because mechanistic thinking is linear and flat, it misses both the micro and macro view that lies above and below. In a survey of planners and

engineers at the 1991 International Transport Conference, they were asked to rate the depth to which they had considered two questions: 'What is the most basic function of the city?' and 'What is the basic function of a transportation system?' They rated the degree to which they had thought about transport 24 per cent higher than the degree to which they had thought about the city.

Yet surely the role of the city is a prior question to understanding the role of transport? It would have been interesting to have asked them to what degree they had thought about the role of a chair in the life of the city. I am sure there would have been a much lower score than for the transport question. They tended to neglect the big picture as well as the detail of the picture.

The eco-relational thinker is interested in both the big picture and the smallest detail because the eco-relational thinker often sees the big picture reflected in the smallest detail. The exchange happening in the Paris street is a microcosm of the whole city. It is the city within the city within the city, what chaos scientists refer to as a fractal arrangement. I am sure you have seen one of those pictures where an artist is standing in front of an easel. On the easel is a picture of the artist standing in front of an easel with a picture of the artist standing in front of an easel – on into infinity. That is a fractal picture. No matter at what scale you view the picture, you have seen the whole picture. In the Paris street scene, a small version of the big picture can be discerned. I did not make deductions *about* the nature of cities from what I saw in the street. I saw the city.

Mono-directional versus multi-directional

Planning 'experts' work from generalisations about the ways cities function, or to be more precise, how some theorist believes they function, down to deductions about how certain actions will affect communities at the neighbourhood level. For example, the big picture which consumes the planner comes from the computer modelling program which predicts traffic in the city will increase by a certain per cent over a particular number of years. They therefore deduce that a particular road in a particular neighbourhood must be upgraded if traffic chaos is to be avoided and quality-of-life preserved.

The eco-relational thinker can also work from the macro down, but, more often than not, works from the bottom up by observing how real life interrelates at the minute neighbourhood level then works outwards to understand the relationships of that neighbourhood life to city life. So, for example, the eco-relational thinker observes a resident in a wheelchair stopped in the roadway talking to a child on a bike and deduces that to increase traffic on that street would upset a delicate balance. This would result in a erosion of quality of life for both the child, the person with the disability and all those who were privileged to witness the scene. The eco-relational thinker, or generalist, then concludes that more efficient ways must be invented (or re-invented) to move people around rather than allowing unrestrained use of private motor vehicles.

Closed versus open
In mechanistic thinking there is a point of arrival – a time when one can say, 'I understand all there is to understand. I have thought it through to its logical conclusion'. In eco-relational thinking there is always another trip around the circle to understand more about life in general.

External versus internal
Machines can be viewed and studied from a detached vantage point. Eco-systems must be experienced. The eco-relational thinker views the big picture, not from outside, but from within the picture, because it is only by becoming part of the event that the complex web of interrelationships can be discerned. Eco-relational thinkers, therefore, spend time reflecting rather than in a blind pursuit of more and more knowledge. They observe life. They probe and delve beneath that which is seen to that which is not seen.

Getting inside the skin

How then does an eco-relational thinker move from outside to inside the picture? The following are five techniques which may provide a start.

Role play
An ecologist in charge of the eradication of mosquitoes responsible for the transmission of Yellow Fever in the coastal cities of Brazil was asked for the secret of his success. 'I try to think like a mosquito,' he replied. In his mind he pretended he was a mosquito looking for a blood meal, a place to mature its eggs, etc.

Eco-relational thinkers trying to find solutions to traffic problems may start by trying to think like all the users of the system: children, those who are elderly or disabled, the mother with a pram, or even the hot-blooded male driver in his red dream-machine. They should also put themselves in the role of a corner store, a seat on the side of the road, or any of the other elements of the Eco-City. As a corner store the role play may start with: 'I am a corner store. I have a quaint but warm atmosphere. What I am about to tell you is the part I play in our little neighbourhood; the things I do well and what people appreciate; my visions for this place; the things that hurt and pain me...'. Through this kind of mental or acted-out role-play a sense of empathy and understanding of the interrelationships begins to emerge.

Questioning observation
Here one takes the time to observe what is happening, then asks questions about the reality that lies behind what is observed. This is the process I used with the Munich chairs. We observe that they are not nailed down and ask why. The key questions are:

- What is the *event* I am observing?
- What are the *relationships* between the elements participating in this event?
- What exchange is taking place between the participants?

Self-awareness
By becoming aware of how you act within a certain situation you become sensitised to how others act. In the case of the Paris chairs, getting inside the skin of those on the seats was relatively easy. I became conscious of what I do when I sit and watch people passing.

Person-to-person interaction
Often the quickest way to discern relationships is to ask those involved

to describe them to you. Here you delve into how a person or group of people interact with their environment. The same three questions used above can be addressed directly to the participants.

Interrogative dialogue

It is also possible to get inside the skin of the inanimate parts of the eco-system. In our minds we can have a dialogue with one of the chairs in the Munich square. What is your relationship to the rest of this square? What relationships do you facilitate? What is your contribution to city life? Why are you not nailed down? What does this reveal about the relationship between you and the city authorities or between you and the citizens? What creative insights have you facilitated? Tell me some of the events you have been an integral part of? Of which are you most proud?

In a similar way we can get inside the skin of the entire eco-system. We can set up a dialogue with a particular city. What potentials do you think you have which are not being realised? What makes you saddest? What makes you the happiest? What things are contributing to your well-being? What things are not? As Jan Tanghe explains, this dialogue may also be with the people of the past:

> Walking around historic towns or villages and looking at important old buildings is not just a matter of collecting a lot of colour slides and going on conducted tours, but should really be a form of dialogue with the people of the past. Such a glimpse into their world is indirectly a matter of thinking about ourselves, and our own buildings and way of living. The architecture and cities of the past are extremely important in the sense that they tell us something about the future we are building: they are just as important as having a searching and first-hand discussion with older people about the 'days gone by'. This teaches us that they lived according to values and ideals which are part of the essence of every human being. These are the values in life which must constantly be renewed, possibly in a more human way, and also be expressed in the buildings which form our surroundings.[7]

If you would like to take one small step toward learning the art of eco-relational thinking try the following experiment. Instead of watching a movie on television, read a book, or spend some time playing with the children, or invite a neighbour over for tea. Spend time reflecting. Delve into the mysteries of life and death. Why not take a walk around your neighbourhood and become more familiar with the people? Become part of the Eco-City – not just a passive watcher. It is only through participation that understanding comes.

Learning to yarn with rubbish bins

Elevation of the role of the generalist and promotion of eco-relational thinking will call for some radical changes in the way children are educated, the way professionals are trained and operate, the way cities are administered and the way decision-making processes are constructed.

Implications for education

The educators in schools and tertiary institutions must cease propagating the now outdated notion of detached, objective scientific observation, which by definition is totally impossible. By isolating a micro-organism and putting it under the microscope, scientists have set up particular *events* in which they are active participants. The scientist, glass slide, microscope and organism have established a particular set of *relationships* and the scientist's objective findings are a record and interpretation of an exchange between all elements, which according to traditional science must exclude those things which can not be 'seen'.

As I have shown from my investigation of chairs, what is seen is only an indication of deeper realities. Lewis Mumford adds: 'How much meaning will be left in the world when the scientific observer eliminates his own subjective contribution? No mechanical system knows the meaning of meaning'.[8]

Education, therefore, needs to change its focus from the accumulation of knowledge to the accumulation of experience and development of the skills needed to interpret and integrate that experience into creative thinking processes.

The training of engineers and town planners, likewise, must take on a life-experience orientation. By living on a busy road for six months a potential town planner may learn more about the effects of transport on neighbourhood life than from four years of tertiary study. One day spent talking to senior citizens about how they accessed the necessities of life before everyone owned cars will suggest solutions to traffic that cannot be found in any text book. A day spent on the buses may reveal more than a semester of lectures.

Town planning and engineering students should be exposed to all the methods of getting inside the 'skin' of the Eco-City including being sent out to document a week in the life of a rubbish bin, a doorway, a chair, a sculpture, a tree, a step, a light pole, or a bus seat. They should be taught how to interrogate these elements and learn from them their role in city life. If they have no role then they can be dispensed with. Hasten the day when we see town planners holding conversations with rubbish bins! Who knows what new insights this may open up.

Implications for the town planning and engineering professions
Adopting eco-relational thinking would change the way planners and engineers view their profession. Instead of seeing themselves as 'mechanics' they would see themselves as 'doctors'. The monkey wrench and slide rule would be replaced with the stethoscope. They would learn the gentle art of placing the stethoscope on the heart of the city and hearing things that are hidden to the uninitiated. The slightest murmur may warn of the onset of a life-threatening disorder that can be nipped in the bud with a little preventative action – a nudge or a wink.

In listening to the heartbeat of neighbourhoods these 'doctors of neighbourhoods' would be searching to understand what promotes life and what takes it away. They would become preoccupied with entirely different questions. What makes this neighbourhood tick? Why is there a sense of togetherness in this street but not in this one? Why does this park work as a people place and not this one? Why is crime high in this neighbourhood but low in this neighbourhood? Is there any connection between traffic flow and the quality of community life?

They would investigate how traffic affects the social fabric; the importance of the corner store; the importance of social mix; the importance of art, fountains and seating in the street. And having understood the delicate balance of the Eco-City, the planner would seek to promote those things which promote life and remove those which do not.

The question, what will the traffic demand be on this road in 20 years time, then becomes redundant. Instead the questions become numerous. How can this public place best be used to enhance the spontaneous life of this neighbourhood and the life of the city? How can we make this space into a place? How can we stop the build-up of traffic on this road from tearing apart this interactive community? All these questions may eventually address the question of future traffic demand, but this becomes a secondary, not primary, consideration.

Planners would cease being mechanics and become prophet/doctors, declaring: 'Push that freeway into the delicate tissue of that neighbourhood and you will kill it'. Engineers would have a competition to find themselves a new name. Econeers maybe?

Implications for administrative structures
When a family engages an architect to help modify their home, the first thing the architect does is discuss with them how the home is used and what functions of living they wish to enjoy which are not currently being accommodated. The architect then uses his or her expertise to draw up a custom-made plan to solve the owner's unique problems. Architects do not take 50 people who want to make changes to their homes,

decipher the common needs and come up with a plan for the greatest common good.

Is it not ludicrous then to have traffic departments or planning departments trying to understand the needs of individual neighbourhoods across a city of a million or more people? Is it not just as ludicrous to have them try to design solutions for neighbourhoods when they have not the first clue about the delicate and intricate workings of that neighbourhood?

One solution to this problem is to break bureaucracies down into administrative districts. These districts would coincide with geographically defined districts in the city and all departments of the city administration would be broken into the same administrative districts and housed together centrally in the district. In this way each person in each department, whether it be traffic, welfare housing or planning, gains an intimate knowledge of the unique workings of the neighbourhoods of their district, just as often happens now in small country towns.

This arrangement also allows for a cross-fertilisation of information and ideas between departments in the same district. It also means that citizens would have a more manageable bureaucracy with which to deal. It would also be important to have a policy of encouraging these public servants to live in the district in which they serve.

Implications for community involvement in decision making

When working on projects, planners and engineers should be required to interact with the community they are planning for. For example, planners should be required to spend 10–25 per cent of their planning time in face-to-face contact with those their planning will effect. Planning bodies may well need to employ permanent 'community interfacers' who can arrange this ongoing contact. This contact must not be in the sterile surrounds of the planner's office, but in people's lounge rooms, gardens and street corners. Arguments that this would add too much to the cost of projects would prove invalid. Costly mistakes would be avoided and, in most cases, the planner would find that the community already has a low-cost innovative solution worked out that will save more than the extra outlay.

There is an old recommendation: when you buy a house do not renovate it until you have lived in it for at least two years. The point of this advice is that you do not know the strengths and weaknesses of a house until you have lived in it. The room that catches the sun during the winter. The room that has too much sun in summer. The directions of the prevailing breezes. The impractical doorways. The little nook that everyone seems to gravitate to. It is the same with a neighbourhood.

It never ceases to amaze me to hear residents talk about their neighbourhoods. They know how intersections work or do not work. They know how things change through the seasons. They know the traffic danger spots and why they are dangerous. It is impossible for planners to plan without this invaluable body of expert opinion. I have heard suggestions from senior citizens that would cost $3,000 to implement and remedy a problem that the council was going to spend $8 million trying to solve.

Besides employing community interfacers, authorities should consider paying communities to employ one or more 'community advocates' who would:

- set up an information gathering network in the community;

- disseminate information that is needed for the community to make an informed decision on issues affecting their neighbourhood;

- facilitate open debate and discussion in the community via information displays, public meetings, newsletters, etc.;

- encourage the community to think laterally and design their own solutions to problems being studied; and

- advocate community concerns and solutions to government departments.

Governments around the world are paying lip service to 'community consultation' but unfortunately, in many cases, it is an expensive exercise in selling a controversial project to a community. Such studies are often a cruel exercise in cynicism, using the veneer of consultation to rob people of their right to plan their own environment. They are a means of shifting the grounds of debate so as to exclude the ordinary citizen. The debate is restricted to one, two or three narrow bands of 'expertise' where the citizen feels out of their depth and at the mercy of those who understand the jargon. The debate becomes purely one of which scheme provides the best technical solution to a problem as perceived and defined by those initiating the study. The true nature of the problem is never part of the study and the 'big picture' is always outside the brief given to the consultants.

Ways must also be found to overcome the strong adversarial structure of modern society and to find new ways to involve everyone as partners in a search for win/win solutions. For example, instead of traditional consultation, why not try mediating a Cooperative Traffic Mitigation Agreement to solve a traffic problem? Ideal areas for such an experiment would be areas suffering from traffic intrusion or areas under threat of major road works where there is already a high awareness of the issues.

A boundary would be drawn around the area and the residents inside this boundary invited to negotiate a Cooperative Traffic Mitigation Agreement with government authorities. This agreement is an acknowledgement that the residents in the affected area are part of the problem; they too drive cars. Their part is to find ways that they can increase the exchange efficiency *within* their neighbourhood; that is, increase exchange while decreasing traffic. This may involve schemes to reduce school traffic, or shopping traffic. For their part the authorities undertake to reduce the traffic coming *through* this particular neighbourhood from outside. This may be in the form of restrictions on truck movements at night, improvements in public transport and narrowing of gateways into the neighbourhood. At both the neighbourhood level and city level, the citizens agree to work with authorities to find lateral ways to improve exchange efficiency.

Such an approach is dependent on all parties thinking in eco-relational terms and all being equal players (although with different skills). If we are to involve everyone in this process including children (yes, they are people and have amazing insights), along with those whose mode of expressions and understanding do not match the rational, abstract, cognitive approach of others, then we will need to design new ways of including them. Many people do not have the capacity to read plans and visualise their end shape or to put their concerns into words. But they can express them in play, paint, clay, models of their neighbourhood which they can manipulate, murals depicting the things they like and dislike about their neighbourhood, and role-plays which help them get inside the skin of their neighbourhood.

Such play becomes yet another important part of Eco-City exchange. Planning the future together is part of the real fabric of cities; productive relationships that enhance the quality of life. Who knows, a day spent in such activities may be more fun than a drive to the beach.

4

Eco-rights

*When society begins to seriously debate social and
environmental rights, the lines for
a constitution of cities will become clearer.*
Kenneth Schneider[1]

*When everything was finished, when our beloved
planet assumed a fairly habitable look, motorists
appeared on the scene...note that the automobile itself
was invented by pedestrians but somehow the motorists
forgot that very quickly. Gentle and intelligent
pedestrians began to get squashed... Roadways were
widened to double their...size, sidewalks
narrowed...pedestrians began to cower in fear against
the walls of buildings.*
Pushkarev and Zupan[2]

*These royal highways – Roman, Persian, Incan, French
– have in common a preference for the straight
perspective, disregarding topography for greater
visibility and shorter alignment... Those royal highways
made it easy only for a certain class in society to come
together...mobility thus fostered the growth of an
effective and powerful ruling group. But the rank and
file, particularly those in the countryside, were doomed
to immobility and to political inaction.*
John Brinckerhoff Jackson[3]

*As western cities have developed, people's accessibility
has been reduced correspondingly; but the reduction
has been unevenly distributed among the population.
The privileged minority who drive cars have about the
same level of access as paupers 150 years ago; the
majority of people are worse off.*
Michael Controy[4]

Human rights in the mechanical city

There is only one way to stop nature from re-asserting its diversity in a mono-culture. The 'weeds' must be chipped and the 'pests' poisoned. Diversity must be suppressed – uniformity rewarded.

The mechanical city automatically infringes human rights whereas the Eco-City automatically promotes human rights. This may appear to be stating the obvious; in the mechanical city humanness becomes subservient to machine functions. But the issue is much deeper than this simple explanation because even the concept of human rights has been affected by our mechanistic thinking. These 'human rights' (the ones heard about most often in Western society) are as different as chalk and cheese from the kinds of human rights that flow from eco-relational thinking and may be termed *eco-rights*.

Changing from mechanistic to eco-relational thinking processes will be the first step in transforming mechanical cities into Eco-Cities. The second step will be an understanding of eco-rights, from which flow the fundamental guidelines for such a reformation.

What then are human rights? According to Leah Levin:

> The concept of human rights has two basic meanings. The first is that inherent and inalienable rights are due to man simply because of being man. They are moral rights which are derived from the humanness of every human being. The second meaning of human rights is that of legal rights, established according to the law-creating process of societies, both national and international. The basis of these rights is the consent of the governed, that is the consent of the subjects of the rights, rather than a natural order, which is the basis of the first meaning.[5]

There are four cornerstones to an eco-relational view of human rights. The first is what the Universal Declaration of Human Rights calls 'the inherent dignity' of all members of the human family. People are not merely a collection of atoms whose value lies in the functions that can be performed by the unique arrangement of those atoms. There is some quality about all members of the human family that gives them inestimable worth. For Charles Birch this something is 'purpose'; the urge not only to live, but also to shape the future.

> The wonder is that life has surmounted the hazards of billions of years to bring us here. Imagine ourselves back some four billion years ago on this planet facing two scenarios: on one side, a vast turbulence, terrific volcanoes belching forth from the inexhaustible fires of the earth's core; on the other side the beginnings of living cells, microscopic, invisible along the water's edge of some shallow sea, quiet, vital. On which are we betting, as in imagination we stand there billions of years ago, volcanoes or life? Life has no credible chance to mean anything against the violent forces of volcano, earthquake, tidal wave and hurricane. Yet we see today

what triumphed – life, spirit, art, music, prophets, martyrs, scientists and saints. The utterly unforeseeable, the unimaginable did happen. The vitality of life is mightier than all the forces of nature waged against it. For us today the perils are horrendous but the possibilities are momentous – all because of the urge that is implanted in life to lead to yet more life.[6]

The second cornerstone is: *all people are born equal.* This does not mean born into equal opportunity but that all are equal in their inherent dignity and worth and therefore have rights to equal shares of the means available to protect, preserve and enhance all facets of their humanness.

The third cornerstone is: *not all people are born into equal opportunity.* If all people came off the end of a production line, all the same gender with exactly the same mass-produced looks in one standard colour, all with identical features, equal physical strength, equal intelligence, equal education, equal material goods, equal ingenuity, and with equal social status there would be no need for human rights. The concept of human 'rights' is in itself an acknowledgement that not all people are born into equal opportunity or with equal assets (natural, bestowed or acquired).

The fourth cornerstone is: *the powerless need protection from those powerful members of society* who wittingly or unwittingly may use their power to oppress the powerless. Inequality of opportunity gives some people greater access to certain commodities (exchange opportunities) such as land, knowledge, means of production, creativity, or money. Control or ownership of these commodities confers certain power which places some people in a position of strength and others in a position of powerlessness. This would not be a problem if we lived in a world where the powerful were totally selfless in using their strength to enrich the powerless. But history proves that there is temptation for the powerful to improve their position at the expense of the powerless – a temptation which is often yielded to. Human rights are therefore necessary to protect the powerless from such exploitation.

Built on these four cornerstones are three basic human rights from which all other rights flow.

Right to protection
The most fundamental of all human rights is that everyone has a right to protection from victimisation by those who are more powerful. Many human rights fall into the category of 'rights to protection'. These can be framed positively or negatively. For example, all people have a right to life; or framed negatively, all people have a right to protection from those who would seek to take their life.

Society has enacted many laws aimed to fulfil the duty of society to protect the powerless against the powerful, protection from false imprisonment, rape, theft, physical assault, assassination of character, child abuse, and racial discrimination.

Right to just distribution

Because all people are born equal in value, no one individual has more rights to the global pool of exchange opportunities which include:

- the resources of the earth which rightfully belong equally to all humanity;

- the resources created by a community, nation or the worldwide community (the 'common-wealth');

- the resources invested in individuals (compassion, knowledge, wisdom, manual skills, etc.).

While the right to protection guards against subtraction, the right to just distribution is concerned with addition. Because not all people are born into equal opportunity, the powerless must be protected from the powerful claiming more than their fair share of the commodities (exchange opportunities) which are available for distribution.

Just distribution is not necessarily equal distribution. Equal distribution would entail ensuring that every person in the world has exactly the same wage, the same land, the same number of knives and forks, the same number of books, the same amount of electricity. Equal distribution would, in fact, be a denial of human rights by denying the uniqueness of each person and the unique resources needed by that person to reach full potential. Taken to a logical conclusion babies would be fed the same meals as adults. Equal distribution does not take account of the unique needs of each person. For example, some love to read, others watch movies.

Just distribution is a far more complex matter. It is the provision of *equal opportunity of access* to the community-generated stockpiles of cultural, social and material commodities so that all who need a particular commodity for their development and enhancement have equal access but with respect to their relative needs. Thus all citizens have equal rights to the electricity generated by a city. Some may choose to use more than others, providing that in the process they do not exhaust the stockpile and cause others to go without. In the event that the city runs low on coal, and electricity is rationed, there will be some citizens that have a right to a greater share than others – for example, those with babies or those whose income may already depend solely on the supply of electricity.

Right to an interactive community

The Universal Declaration of Human Rights recognises that people can only reach their full potential if nourished by an interdependent or interactive community. Article 29 states: 'Everyone has duties to the community in which alone the free and full development of his *[sic]* personality is possible'.

People can only reach their full potential if nourished by what other humans give: love, protection, a shoulder to cry on, art, culture, information, wisdom, friendship, food, clothing etc. Denial of these 'gifts' is not only to deny people the essential nutrients for their health and flowering, it may endanger their very survival.

This right to a positive, interactive community is also implied in Article 22 of the Universal Declaration.

> Everyone, as a member of society, has the right...and is entitled to realisation, through national effort and international cooperation and in accordance with the organisation and resources of each State, of the economic, social and cultural rights indispensable for his *[sic]* dignity and the free development of his *[sic]* personality.

But rights bring responsibilities – a duty to give whatever gifts are needed so others may also be nourished. Thus Article 19 ties together the duty, 'everyone has duties to the community', with the right, 'in which alone the free and full development of his *[sic]* personality is possible'.

To acknowledge that all people are not born with equal opportunity is to acknowledge that we are not all born with equal 'gifts' or assets. We are not all brilliant artists, orators, care givers, or lovers. But all have a duty to share the gifts they do have because, as trite as it may sound, all humanity is the poorer if they are withheld. By the withholding of these gifts, others are robbed of their right to an asset they need for their full development. There is an inherent duty on the powerful to use their strength to strengthen the powerless. The powerless in becoming powerful, will in turn strengthen the powerful. This is what is meant by *interactive* community or what has previously been called an Eco-City.

Many people in the Western world think of rights in a very individualistic way – *my* rights – the trump card that allows them to do their own thing. These are the 'rights' that emanate from the mechanical city. If we are to be honest and accept René Descartes' view that 'the material universe is a machine and nothing but a machine' – a view that led eventually to the establishment of the mechanical city – then there are no human rights. Machine parts do not have rights. Human rights are simply a convenient charade under which to amass more power. Thus a planner once denounced my presentation at a conference by insisting that he had the *right* to live on a quarter-acre block and he had the *right* to drive his car where and when he wanted. These kinds of 'rights' are always in opposition to other people's 'rights' – in this case the right for those without access to a car to enjoy equal levels of exchange. Invariably in this war of rights, the powerful win.

Many writers, particularly those from the Third World or non-Western cultures have been very wary of the current discussion of rights because they see them as a means of overriding collective goals of national and international prosperity or security. This is because this third element, the right to an interactive community, has been left out of the discussion. It counters the mechanistic use of rights as a means of gaining power.

The right to an interactive community is therefore the life-blood of human rights. Individual rights can only be realised in the context of a healthy, functioning community of interdependence. Personal growth and prosperity are inextricably tied to community growth and prosperity (I use prosperity in its wider meaning, not just monetary). When the powerful oppress the powerless they do violence to themselves. As Saul Alinsky wrote:

> A major revolution to be won in the immediate future is the dissipation of man's illusion that his own welfare can be separated from all others... Concern for our private, material well-being with disregard for the well-being of others is...stupidity worthy of the lower animals. It is man's foot still dragging in the primeval slime of his beginnings... The record of the past centuries has been a disaster, for it was wrong to assume that man would pursue morality on a level higher than his day-to-day living demanded; it was a disservice to the future to separate morality from man's daily desires and elevate it to a plane of altruism and self-sacrifice. The fact is that it is not man's 'better nature' but his self-interest that demands that he be his brothers keeper... I believe man is about to learn that the most practical life is the moral life and that the moral life is the only road to survival.[7]

Rights are essentially about relationships and cannot be understood outside that context. Relationships always involve two or more individuals or elements. Wherever one person has a right, another has a duty. This right–duty relationship can only be realised in an interactive community or Eco-City.

For example, consider the issue of safety. Protection from assault is a basic human right, but who is to do the protecting? The greatest deterrent to crime is eyes on the street. As trust is established between the residents of a street they begin to police their own neighbourhood. People watch out for each other and take responsibility for each other. But this neighbourhood policing only comes about after people have established a trust which is the result of numerous casual contacts. It does not happen to the same extent in tenement housing estates where there is a rapid turnover of people or in anonymous, dormitory suburbs.

Recently a friend of mine awoke at two in the morning to the sound of a noisy car driving slowly up the street. He heard it stop around the corner. The friend became suspicious because he knew by its sound that the car did not belong to anyone in the street. So he went to the window to investigate and saw three youths breaking into a neighbour's car. He yelled out and they ran off. My friend thus fulfilled his duty to protect the property rights of his neighbour. But what enabled him to do so was his relationship with his neighbours. He knew them so well he recognised the sound of a stranger's car. It is interesting to note that this instance provided an opportunity for relationships and trust to be further strengthened in the neighbourhood which further heightened the sense of duty neighbours felt to each other.

Do trees have rights?

The above description of rights demonstrates how deeply mechanistic thinking has seeped into our consciousness and how hard it will be to root it out. It is obvious that seeing the city as an eco-system had an effect on the way I perceived human rights. But in a sense my perceptions are still largely mono-dimensional; I have only looked at the relationships that exist between people. What of the relationships between people and animals? Or people and trees? Or people and their city? Or people and chairs? Surely all of these are part of the eco-system. By omission I have reduced the non-human elements of the eco-system to tools or things for the betterment of homo-sapiens.

One of the challenges for the future will be to apply eco-relational thinking further to this issue of rights and to evolve a more comprehensive concept of eco-rights. In the meantime we can start with a series of acknowledgements. We can acknowledge that just as we are dependent for our life on what others can give, we are equally dependent on the elements of our environment which in the past we considered dispensable or of little worth. We can also acknowledge the 'life force' where it exists. In the passage quoted earlier from Birch, he talks of the 'vitality of life' which has triumphed over all the odds. 'Living cells, microscopic, invisible along the water's edge of some shallow sea' pitted against 'volcanoes belching forth from the inexhaustible fires of the earth's core'. We kid ourselves if we believe that this 'urge that is implanted in life to lead to yet more life' mysteriously came into existence at some point in the development of humanity. It has been there in nature from the very beginning. Even the smallest micro-organisms have a will to survive, enhance their quality of life, and somehow play their part in the great unfolding drama of the universe. This may not be in a conscious way but is innate to their very nature. As such they too deserve special honour.

Cars on streets: right or privilege?

For over 10,000 years, streets in cities belonged to the people for social interaction, recreation and to provide access to people, goods and places. Beasts of burden were allowed on the streets provided they did not bite or constitute a danger to life or limb of other road users.

Today, by default, society has granted freedom of the streets to a beast of burden which annually kills 250,000 to 500,000 people and maims millions more. Also, the carcinogenic gases that rise from the automobile excreta kill an estimated 30,000 people in the US alone,[8] are killing the forests of Europe, cause crop losses of $1.9 billion to $4.5 billion for just four cash crops in the US,[9] and are not only degrading marine life in the Atlantic coastal waters but are also the major human-made contributor to the greenhouse effect. As well, the sounds these new beasts make chase people from the streets and sometimes, even from their homes. Many people who cannot escape are literally sent crazy by the noise. As well as having a ferocious appetite for fuel these new beasts occupy almost three times more space (for parking) than the space occupied by their owner's home.[10]

The facts are that the automobile was never granted rights to the streets. It took them by stealth. When the car first appeared it was viewed purely as a leisure vehicle for the rich. When on public roads, cars had to proceed at walking pace with a man in front waving a red flag. In 1901, Mercedes Benz estimated that the ultimate world market would never be higher than one million cars. But during the Twenties, with the

introduction of mass-production technology, the culture of the car took root and it changed from leisure vehicle to beast of burden. At the time there was no serious debate as to whether the 10,000 year tradition of refusing right of access to beasts which kill and maim should be reversed. It is now time this topic was seriously discussed.

There is a strong moral argument, pursued mainly by European environmentalists, that freedom to use the highways was recognised as a basic right long before the invention of the motor car. Therefore, when motor cars restrict the right of others to use the roadway then it is the car that must yield to the former's right. As one writer has commented: 'It is possible to take the view that there is no natural right, and never should be, to take motor vehicles into public places, and permission to do so should be regarded as a privilege...'.[11]

Now I can imagine those who worship their automobiles becoming very upset, dusting off their history books and quoting long passages about the intolerable levels of horse traffic in some medieval city. To quote one source:

> The Strand of those days...was the throbbing heart of the people's essential London... But the mud! And the noise! And the smell!... The whole of London's crowded wheeled traffic – which in parts of the city was at times dense beyond movement – was dependent on the horse... A more assertive mark of the horse was the mud [a euphemism] that, despite the activities of a numerous corps of red-jacketed boys who dodged among the wheels and hooves with pan and brush in service to iron bins at the pavement-edge...flooded the streets with churnings of 'pea soup' that at times collected in pools overbrimming the kerb... And after the mud the noise, which, again endowed by the horse, surged like a mighty heart-beat in the central districts of London's life. It was a thing beyond all imaginings.[12]

Obviously London had problems. The horse had taken over some of the streets. The problems caused by horses may well have been just as intolerable as the problems caused by traffic in our modern cities. That being the case it may be possible that horses, by sheer weight of numbers, were causing an injustice to be done. In this situation the problem was one of numbers – not necessarily the nature of the beast.

This gives an important clue in understanding how modern-day vehicles infringe basic human rights. While this section started with a tirade against the new beast of burden (designed to shake some people free of their irrational worship of the beast), the infringement of human rights is not due solely to the inherent nature of the beast. In some cases a single vehicle may be the cause of an infringement of someone's rights but in most cases it is the quantity of vehicles, coupled with their inherent nature, that produces the infringement. In a city of one million people, one person choosing to drive to work instead of taking the bus will not induce city spread, or run down public transport and exchange opportunities. But if 100,000 people make that choice at eight o'clock each morning then a chain of events is set up and the result is a clear contravention of other people's basic human rights. Each one of these 100,000 people must take some responsibility for the resulting infringement of rights and should not become upset if society repeals or limits what has become an infringement of rights.

If society had thought through the eventual consequences of allowing that first motorised vehicle to use the streets, it may well have decided the eventual costs would outweigh the benefits and refused to grant permission. On the other hand, society may have granted permission, but on the understanding that this was a privilege – not a right – that could be withdrawn at any time.

It is important to re-state that I am not anti-car *per se.* That would be reactionary. However, I recognise that society has established a transport system which is a complex interplay of factors but which clearly discriminates against the powerless members of that society – much like the complex interplay involved in the international monetary system. For example, there may be nothing intrinsically wrong with coffee beans. But when poor subsistence farmers in Third World countries are forced to grow cash crops such as coffee for the rich First World, instead of growing traditional crops to feed their families, and when the money they receive from the cash crops is insufficient to buy enough food, then the humble coffee bean has become part of an arrangement that causes poor people to starve while the rich enjoy a luxury drink. The solution may be to either stop drinking coffee or to change the system.

It could be argued that while the car remained a leisure vehicle in small numbers, and while it travelled at a speed that did not endanger other road users, there was no problem. Exhaust emissions were too low to harm people's health. The noise was not much more than that produced by a noisy group of children. And no-one's exchange opportunities were reduced. A plausible case could have been made to defend the right of vehicles to use public highways between villages, provided they travelled in a manner calculated not to cause loss of life or limb. But when society created a transport system where there were winners and losers, and the losers were those at the bottom of the economic ladder, then an injustice was perpetrated which must be redressed.

The three basic levels of human rights: right to protection, right to just distribution and right to an interactive community, have implications for the issue of traffic in cities.

Right to protection

The right to protection has three clear applications to traffic. Firstly, it is clear that once a person is behind the steering wheel of a car they are in a position of strength, exactly the same as being armed with a weapon. There is, therefore, a moral obligation for society to enact laws or make physical changes to the environment to protect the powerless (the unarmed) from being victimised by those who are stronger. This means protection for the pedestrian, cyclist, resident and the public transport user.

Secondly, protection is a right against subtraction. The erosion of home territory, 'placeness', spontaneous exchange opportunities and the removal of other exchange opportunities (e.g. corner stores, parks) must clearly be seen as a subtraction for those who do not have the means to compensate for these losses. Similarly, the removal of quietness, the removal of clean air and the removal of safety are a 'theft' of elements essential for people's well-being.

Thirdly, all the residents of a city (motorists and non-motorists) may need protection from the powerful road construction lobby, the car manufacturing lobby and the bureaucrats whose status and income depends on a spreading automobile empire.

Right to just distribution

This right was defined as 'providing equal opportunity of access to the community-generated stockpiles of cultural, social and material commodities...'. Transportation is not only one of these commodities, but is also one of the chief means by which people gain access to almost all the other cultural, social and material commodities: friends, art galleries, material goods, churches, recreational facilities, libraries, schools, clubs, protest rallies, and government offices. It is therefore impossible to have a just distribution of cultural, social and material goods, as called for in the Universal Declaration of Human Rights, unless there is also equal opportunity of access to transportation. This may well mean placing restrictions on some members of society if the means they choose to gain access limit the ability of others to access their fair share of exchange opportunities from the community stockpile.

Right to an interactive community

Traffic reduces opportunity for social interaction and neighbourhood life. It cuts off the very roots that carry the 'nutrients' which are absolutely essential for the full social and cultural development of people. It stops both the giving and receiving which is the essential life-force of an interactive community. In a real sense, traffic not only contravenes specific human rights (rights to protection and rights to a just distribution) but also diminishes the very context in which these human rights can be maintained. In fact, it attacks the very means by which *all* rights in the Universal Declaration of Human Rights can be fulfilled. Excessive traffic, therefore, can paralyse the very heart of human rights.

I started this discussion on rights by saying there were two kinds of rights; moral rights and legal rights. Wherever a community sees basic human rights being contravened it is a duty of that community to enact laws that will protect against this contravention. As J.G. Diefenbaker, chief promoter of the 1960 Canadian Bill of Rights, said in 1947: 'The great traditional rights are mere pious ejaculations unless the individual has the right to assert them in the courts of law'.[13]

Most countries have enacted laws that partly recognise the obligation to protect citizens against traffic. These include speed limits, blood alcohol limits, exhaust emission limits and vehicle design specifications to minimise damage to pedestrians if they are struck. *But there are virtually no laws to protect residents from having their exchange opportunities diminished or their space for social interaction stolen.*

These potential new laws must be enforceable, realistic and must provide mechanisms for implementation. There has to be a fundamental shift in position from which the laws are drafted, as fundamental as a shift from presumption of guilt to presumption of innocence. While owning an automobile may be a right, taking it into a public place must be seen as a privilege, which may or may not be granted. And this is only after society is certain that granting the privilege will not contravene basic eco-rights.

The introduction of new laws will not in itself be enough to reverse the injustices which have already become entrenched in auto-dominated cities. A complex interplay of issues has to be addressed by society and, ultimately, by governments. Auto-induced injustices are intimately connected to other urban issues and can only be tackled by taking a holistic view of urban life.

For example, part of the solution will be government initiatives that encourage the desegregation of suburbs and support mixed socio-economic suburbs. The segregation of suburbs inevitably leads to injustice, malapportionment of resources and entrenchment of discrimination against the powerless. Because the environment we live in largely shapes our world view, this segregation also creates the illusion that this is the way the world should be.

Hugh Stretton explains why he believes governments should encourage greater residential mixtures and should absolutely prohibit large-scale low-income segregations. He argues that residential mix is of direct social benefit to both the poor and the rich.

Besides taking each other's children to the speed-car track and the theatre, there are more important exchanges of ambition, compassion, and the learning and initiative required to use whatever social services are in theory offering. From poorer neighbours, affluent children may pick up better politics, mechanical skills and social capacities than their snobbish schools offer them...

Residential segregations are steady and potent enemies of all equalities – including the most sacred and official equalities. Mixed suburbs can distribute municipal services equally to unequal rate-payers, but segregated suburbs make sure the poor get only what they pay for – including, sometimes, the municipal councillors. Segregation usually unequalizes people's access to open spaces – to parks, views, well-kept playgrounds and playing fields, sometimes rivers and beaches. It can often unequalize peace and quiet and fresh air... Segregation sometimes unequalizes the safety of the streets, always their beauty and cleanliness...

Mixture, on the other hand, is one of the simplest, cheapest and least oppressive ways of reducing the effects of other inequalities... There can be no doubt of the interest which the poorer half of society has in mixing with the richer half. Any district can use a thick sprinkling of able, obstinate succeeders, helping to keep the local councillors honest, resisting pressurized re-zonings and philistine road builders, chaining themselves to menaced trees, paying for planning appeals and hectoring the local M.P.; organising local branches of the political parties; agitating for kindergartens, parks, playgrounds and libraries, and showing how to use and criticise and improve them; paying good rates for these good things. The same sprinkling of affluence can make a critical difference to the quality and variety of service and social activity that the district can support communally or attract commercially... Such better services enlarge everybody's choices. They also help to equalise opportunities.[14]

It becomes obvious why it is of critical importance to understand the effects of mixed, as opposed to segregated, neighbourhoods if society wants to create a transport system which provides equal opportunity of access to a wide range of facilities, services and goods. Encouraging mixed neighbourhoods will not only create a more equitable distribution of facilities, services and goods, it will also provide a fairer distribution of the means of going to these facilities, such as bikeways, walkways, and public transport.

Stretton brings me back full circle to what I described earlier as the life-blood and heart of human rights, the right to an interactive community. Auto-induced injustices cannot be addressed unless governments encourage and create the climate in which interactive communities can grow and flourish. And these interactive communities must contain a full social range of people. In new residential developments the task is relatively easy – if governments control the development process and thread government housing (making sure it does not look like government housing) through all new residential areas. Each new community should have all types of housing: walk-up flats, cheap speculative housing, special purpose housing for the aged, housing for university students and prestigious housing.

Moving those who are poor into wealthier enclaves is relatively easy, as simple as buying houses and making them available to low-income families or building town houses or units for the aged. What will be difficult is convincing the existing residents that such moves will not erode the value of their properties but will rather enrich their neighbourhood.

Moving the upwardly mobile into poorer communities is harder, but perhaps not impossible. If authorities anticipate areas that are about to be gentrified (the conversion of former slum/working class areas into 'smart suburbs') then they must act to safeguard the traditional housing of the poor while leaving room for others to move in.

Authorities must also identify areas that are currently segregated and make these a priority for establishing facilities and services that will attract higher income people and will encourage locals to stay on. Part of this process may be a deliberate effort to change the image of an area by sponsoring cultural activities and festivals which are rooted in the locality.

Raw end of the deal

The amount of road space to be provided in a city is not an engineering question. It is first and foremost a question of social justice. Auto-dominated cities create a group of people we may call 'access-to-exchange disadvantaged' (ATED). People who are ATED are often elderly, poor, disadvantaged, handicapped, children, parents without access to a second car and those who choose not to own a car. Between 40 and 60 per cent of the population in most Western cities are ATED. Each increase in road infrastructure discriminates against this group in seven distinct ways. Some have already been discussed but here they are brought together to complete the picture.

■ Loss of access to exchange opportunities through a run down in public transport
Trying to service a number of people spread over a large area obviously costs more than servicing the same number spread over a smaller area. The spreading-city syndrome undermines the viability of public transport.

For people who are ATED, the only way they can gain independent access to a desirable destination outside walking or cycling range is via shared rides or public transport. Therefore, unless counter measures are taken, any increase in road infrastructure further undermines their ability to access exchange opportunities. While some people may like to argue whether or not the motorist gains new levels of exchange, one thing is plain; each increase in road infrastructure widens the gap between people who are ATED and non-ATED.

For example, Brisbane once had a tram system with a frequency as high as eight minutes. The trams were removed because they slowed the car traffic. Today, average journey times for cars have remained relatively static but public transport frequency has dropped from eight minutes to 20 or 30 minutes. Public transport users have clearly lost in the attempt (albeit unsuccessful) to improve conditions for motorists. At the same time, motorists have clogged the roads causing massive delays to public transport.

■ Loss of access to exchange opportunities through loss of walking and cycling space

Increasing road infrastructure decreases walking and cycling space by either taking it over for roads or allowing it to fall into traffic's zone-of-influence. Any increase in road space for motorists is a decrease in walking and cycling space for everyone, but again, the hardest hit are people who are ATED. They do not have the option of driving when walking and cycling become impossible or too dangerous.

■ Loss of exchange opportunities through city sprawl and loss of local facilities
People who are ATED have their available means of transport seriously eroded. In addition, because the whole physical layout and structure of the city is changed to suit the car, they are forced to travel further to reach the same number of destinations.

Neighbourhood stores and local facilities are the first victims of the automobile's spreading empire. For the motorists, the compensation for this loss of convenience may be that, at the regional shopping centre, they have a greater range and prices are 'cheaper'. But spare a thought for those without access to a car. They cannot simply hop in their car and drive four kilometres to the nearest convenience store when they run out of milk. Nor can they take a weekly drive along the freeway to the regional shopping centre, load one or two weeks supply of groceries into the boot of their car, then drive back along the freeway, park the car and carry the groceries the final ten metres to the kitchen. Instead, they must walk to the nearest bus stop and wait for a bus (if indeed there is public transport going anywhere near the shopping centre). After doing their shopping they must sit and wait for the next bus. They have not bought any frozen goods because they know they will be spoilt by the time they reach home and they did not buy any luxury goods because the bare necessities weigh as much as they know they will be able to carry home from the bus stop. On the journey home they can contemplate how on earth they will cross the six lanes of traffic with all these bags when the bus lets them off – particularly if a bag has started to tear. Thus, increasing road infrastructure not only limits the exchange opportunities of people who are ATED, but impinges on their whole quality of life.

Another example is the centralising or loss of play space for children. Instead of them being able to simply walk out their front door and have an informal game of cricket in the street, children must join a cricket club and be driven each Saturday or Sunday to a specialised field – that is if their family is not also ATED.

■ Trip suppression and loss of independent mobility
When the transport environment becomes too hostile, many people simply withdraw and do not make a trip they would like to make. Several examples have been given that illustrate this point; the elderly couple who stopped visiting friends on the other side of the road because the road became too busy and Appleyard's study where people on Heavy street had stopped visiting each other. I saw three wheelchairs on the streets in Groningen and none in Los Angeles.

In Groningen, and other pedestrian- and cycle-friendly cities, the streets feel as if they belong to people. The streets make you want to jump on your bike or into your wheelchair and go exploring. In Los Angeles, traffic rules the streets. The traffic screams at the non-motorists that they are not welcome and should stay at home.

A travel characteristics study done in Brisbane showed that between 1976 and 1986 the number of trips per household for high income earners (49 per cent of population) increased by 11 per cent while the number of trips made by low income households (23 per cent of population) suffered a 9 per cent drop.[15] While the rich are now going to the beach more often because there is a new freeway, the elderly and poor have stopped visiting their friends or playing lawn bowls because it is too dangerous to walk or because public transport is too infrequent.

The plight of children is of special concern. Auto-dominance erodes the independent mobility of children. Recently my daughter's class at school had to talk to their parents about what life was like when they were children. The children then wrote a piece to be put on a poster entitled 'Our Dreams For The Future'. The two things that featured prominently were firstly the environment (trees, deserts, and pollution), and secondly traffic and independent mobility.

> When my mum was little she was allowed to go to the park and to the shop by herself. We can't go somewhere by ourselves because there is too much traffic...

> Mum could stay on the road with her friends because there were not many cars on the road...

> My mum and dad could walk at night and play on the road. I can not because it is...*dangerous.*

While all children are ATED and therefore suffer this loss of independent mobility, it is again the children of parents who are also ATED who suffer most. Parents with access to a car drive their kids to play with friends. But the children of the ATED must simply stay at home.

■ Forced to bear an unfair share of environmental and social costs
Those who are elderly, poor, or disabled in our society often suffer a double disadvantage. Not only are their own mobility and exchange opportunities reduced by traffic and traffic induced city spread, but they are also forced to pay the major costs of other people's mobility. It is a fact of life that those who can afford a car can also usually afford to buy a house divorced from its negative effects. It is true that 'the social costs of freeways fall on the poor'.[16]

Think for a moment. Who would want to live on a major road and endure the noise, the air pollution, the invasive grime, the unsafe environment for their children, the restricted access to their property, the parking restrictions and a degraded outlook? Not many people if they had a genuine choice. Those who live on Heavy street are the trapped residents who, through age, sentiment or financial situation, cannot flee. It is the poor and disadvantaged who either buy or rent here because they cannot afford to live anywhere else or because there is nothing else available. And it is they who are the first to be uprooted when roads are widened so the more affluent can still drive their cars to work in the city centre. Does that seem fair?

The social and environmental costs are not superficial. They are the kind of costs that help reinforce the cycles of disempowerment that put these people where they are. Studies have shown, for example, that children exposed to constant and excessive noise have their development slowed.[17] Lead from petrol can also cause intellectual impairment. The opportunity for these children to socialise and explore their neighbourhood is limited. A neighbourhood with noisy, dirty arterials is not the kind of environment in which one expects people to dream new dreams and break the cycles that keep them powerless.

- ■ **Cost of transport increased**
  Ian Manning concludes in *Beyond Walking Speed* that the main achievement in Australian urban transport over the past century has been to 'replace low speed, low cost transport with high speed, high cost transport'.[18] The two steps in this replacement process were

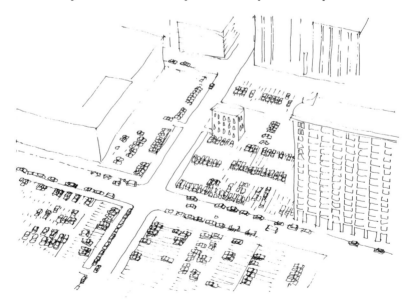

replacing walking (basically free) with public transport (moderate cost) and then replacing public transport with private motor vehicles (high cost). As I mentioned earlier, Manning shows that this achievement of high speed transport has not resulted in shorter journey times. Because people have exchanged low cost transport for high cost transport, we are now paying a greater share of our income to make the same trips our ancestors did without any significant gains in time or exchange opportunities.

One wonders who then has benefited. This new arrangement may be of little consequence to those who own cars even ignoring the effect it may have on their children or spouse. If we are fool enough to pay more for the same, so be it. At least our high-cost transport machine is a status symbol. But again it is those without constant, direct access to a car, including the young, who suffer the most.

The replacement of low speed, low cost transport with high speed, high cost transport has all the hallmarks of the infant milk formula scandals in Third World countries. Once seduced into trying the formula, the mother loses a supply of better quality milk which was virtually free and has to divert money from the necessities of life to pay for an inferior product. To put it bluntly, with transport, the poor are being forced to divert essential income to something that was once free and what they receive in exchange is inferior.

■ International oppression

While this book concentrates more on the effects of the car on the city and on individuals in the city, those in the Western world seem intent on exporting the injustices of a car culture. Third World governments are believing the propaganda about the freedom and prosperity that comes with an auto-dominated economy.

In 1989, officials in Jakarta banned becaks, a three-wheeled cycle-rickshaw, 'because they were the main cause of increasing traffic congestion'.[19] For some of Jakarta's poor this not only resulted in the loss of their job, they also lost their home and their savings. For them the becak represented all three.

Similarly, authorities in Dakha in Bangladesh announced plans in 1987 to ban pedicabs even though they employed more than 100,000 people. Recently the World Bank issued a massive report on transport in China which did not even mention the word 'bicycle'. As a result, Chinese planners like Min Fengkui are calling for cycle traffic to be strictly controlled 'with the ultimate intention of reducing it to an auxiliary means of short-range transport'. Min holds up the relegation of the bicycle in the West to 'sport and recreation' as 'our preference in the planning of our future urban development'.[20] As Michael

Replogle writes:

> Decisions on transport policy are usually in the hands of technocrats – engineers and economists, often Western-educated, who are wealthy enough to own cars. They are backed by urban elites who profit from oil import deals, car dealerships or construction contracts.[21]

To reinforce this move towards an auto-culture, Western countries often tie aid to planning for motorised traffic or the construction of road infrastructure. Between 1972 and 1985, rail and bus systems received less than one-third of the funding for World Bank urban transportation projects.

This priority of aid has a dramatic effect on the poor in these countries. It helps to construct an infrastructure that becomes a continuing source of oppression. In Haiti, for example, only one out of every 200 people owns a car, yet one-third of the country's import budget is devoted to fuel and transportation equipment. Every dollar diverted to support the illusion of increasing mobility for the rich elite is a dollar that could have been spent on food, shoes, bicycles or public transport for the poor. The net result of car-centred development according to Michael Replogle is to boost imports, increase foreign debt and make life worse for the poor.[22]

The over-developed industrial countries have become 'energy gluttons'. North America, Western Europe, Japan and Oceania account for only 16 per cent of the world's population but 88 per cent of car production and 81 per cent of the global fleet. China and India with 38 per cent of the world's population had scarcely one half of one per cent.[23]

This section began with the assertion that the level of road infrastructure is not only an engineering question; it is first and foremost a question of social justice. However, it is more than that. It is a question of redressing injustice already done. It is intolerable that it is the powerless members of a society, those least able to defend themselves, who are not only forced to pay the social and environmental costs of the travel of the powerful, but at the same time are forced to sacrifice some of their own travel opportunities. The greatness of any city can be judged by the way it treats its weakest member. Humanity and the environment stand as a single unit and when we do violence to our environment we do violence to ourselves.

A draft charter of access-to-exchange rights

After I speak at public meetings people often express a dual sense of excitement and hopelessness: 'While you have inspired us to see new possibilities for our city, I can't see things ever changing in my lifetime'. Such a sense of hopelessness is based on historical short-sightedness. History is littered with major revolutions in thinking and values. One does not need to look too far into the past to find examples of rapid attitudinal change; there was even a time when Christians bought slaves.

I always ask people if they remember the days of smoke-filled offices and aircraft and the Bugger-Up Society (an anonymous group of anti-smoking campaigners who spray-painted witty slogans on cigarette billboards in the dead of the night). Ten years ago no-one in Australia would have forecast the incredible changes in public attitude toward smoking in public places. Anyone who suggested that legislation would be introduced that banned all cigarette advertising, banned smoking in workplaces, taxis, aircraft and numerous other public places would have been considered naive in the extreme. A government that dared to introduce these measures would have been voted out of office.

What caused this overnight revolution in values? It was that a new concept took root in the collective mentality: people have a right not to be forced to breath other people's smoke. A similar revolution in attitudes will take place when notions of traffic-related abuses of human rights enter the collective consciousness. One way of hastening the education process may be the declaration of a *Bill of Access-to-Exchange Rights.* Some inclusions for such a bill are discussed here. Appendix A is a suggested first draft which is presented for detailed community debate.

Equitable distribution
People are entitled to the protection of their right to a just and equitable share of the exchange opportunities which a city can provide. No group or person should be allowed to improve its share of these exchange opportunities at the expense of another group or person unless this action is necessary to right an existing unjust distribution.

Unless countermeasures are taken to maintain existing levels of accessibility, increasing road infrastructure in existing urban areas automatically decreases exchange opportunities for people who are ATED. Counter measures would include maintaining public transport services at pre-auto level, building safe walk and cycleways where existing walk and cycle space has been eroded or subjugated; and either giving back the local facilities which are lost through road widening or upgrading alternative means of transport to the nearest like facility. The costs of all these 'improvements', which are needed simply to maintain the levels of exchange for people who are ATED, must be borne by motorists not by the victims. Motorists have chosen to use private transport rather than the collectively provided means of transport.

While those who are ATED have suffered the greatest loss of exchange opportunities, the supreme irony of auto-dominated cities is that the wheel has turned full circle and those who once sought to improve their levels of exchange by driving their cars on bigger and better roads have now had their own accessibility diminished by other motorists trying to do the same. In most large cities it now takes longer to drive to work than it would if everyone went by public transport and motorists must therefore bear all the costs their choice imposes on the rest of society.

Preferential treatment for pedestrians and cyclists

Pedestrians and cyclists have a right to preferential treatment over motorised traffic for funding, access rights and space. Where private motorists are granted the privilege of sharing street space with pedestrians and cyclists, the pedestrian and cyclist have right of way over private motor vehicles at all times.

Stephen Plowden, author of the authoritative *Towns Against Traffic*, cites three common-sense reasons why pedestrians and cyclists should be given preferential treatment over private motorists.

> Other things being equal, one should presumably start with the principle that all travellers have equal rights, regardless of the means by which they choose to travel. But since travellers by motor vehicles are better armed and better protected than pedestrians and cyclists they tend to take priority whenever any conflict arises. One aim of policy should be to correct this bias. Moreover, from the general social point of view, other things are not all equal. Pedestrians and cyclists are much cheaper to accommodate than motor vehicles and do no environmental harm. This is a strong reason for giving them not merely equal, but preferential treatment.[24]

There are many other common-sense reasons why pedestrians and cyclists should have priority for funding, space and access. A fitter population would result in a reduced medical bill for society. Walking and cycling encourages a greater level of social interaction and gives the city a more relaxed, friendly feeling.

But all these are common-sense reasons rather than moral arguments. Plowden touches one of the moral arguments when he says that because motorists are better armed and better protected they tend to take precedence and one of the aims of policy should be to correct this bias. One of the roles of human rights is to protect the powerless against oppression by the strong, in this case the pedestrian and cyclist against the better equipped motorist. Because each increase in provision for motor cars brings a corresponding reduction in cycling and pedestrian space and reduction in exchange opportunity, the strong are gaining at the expense of the weak. There is therefore a moral imperative on society to protect the traditional right of access to streets and roads for pedestrians and cyclists.

Another moral argument is that walking and cycling infrastructure provides a more just distribution of exchange opportunities than infrastructure for private motor vehicles. Because a much greater proportion of society can walk or cycle than can drive, placing priority on walk and cycle facilities provides a larger part of the population with equality of opportunity for access to social, material and cultural goods.

Where pedestrians, cyclists and private motorists use common road space, the pedestrian and cyclist should have right of way over private motor vehicles at all times. I have argued that pedestrians and cyclists have a prior claim to road space. This is not to say that society may not set aside special space for private motor vehicles, but that where motor vehicles, pedestrians and cyclists are forced to share road space, the pedestrians and cyclists have prior claim.

Right to access
No resident should be denied access to community and public facilities simply because of economic or social status, age, sex or physical condition.

In many cities, the physical arrangement of roads and facilities is such that only those who own cars have access.

Rights for public transport users
Public transport users have a right not to be unduly hindered, delayed or have their service downgraded by private motorists.

When motorists transfer from public to private transport, they not only cause a revenue drop which effects the standard of service which can be provided, they clog up the roads which imposes time delays on the public transport user (bus and tram). What right do these people have to cause the downgrading and slowing of the only form of transport some people have for the longer trip?

Right to not have to pay other people's costs
No person should be forced because of station in life to bear an unequal share of the social, environmental or monetary costs of other people's travel.

This right not only applies to those who live on major roads; it applies to all people. Those who choose to drive rather than walk, cycle or take public transport, impose on the rest of the community, including those on quiet streets, social, environmental and monetary costs which include: a decrease in exchange opportunities due to a more spread-out city, loss of local neighbourhood facilities, and the marooning of facilities in a sea of traffic and car parks; a decrease in spontaneous exchange opportunities because of decrease in walking and cycling space and run down of public transport; a disruption of friendship links; a destruction of city 'soul' and placeness as the rich diversity of living spaces is diluted; an increase in rates and taxes as the city becomes more inefficient due to urban sprawl (roads, electricity, water, drainage, public transport cost more per head); an overall deterioration in air quality; and a greater chance of being killed or seriously injured.

Of course, those who live on busy streets pay all these costs plus more: a greater restriction on friendship links; a greater loss of community play space; a higher level of noise intrusion; a greater shrinkage of home territory; all pervasive exhaust and tyre dust; difficulty entering and leaving the driveway and loss of parking; a hostile atmosphere; and a physical loss of part or whole of property for road widening.

It may be argued that society already compensates people who live on or near major roads by offering cheaper rents and home prices. This argument ignores the plight of the trapped resident. It also ignores the fact that the cheaper rent or house price does not offer the poorer person a true choice, it is simply a mechanism of exploitation. The prices of houses, which are divorced from the social and environmental effects of the car, are set at a level which cannot be afforded by this group. By this mechanism the 'haves' can force the 'have-nots' to pay the major share of the environmental, social and health costs of the 'haves' travel.

Arguing that no person should be forced to pay the monetary costs of other people's travel raises the prickly problem of non-motorists subsidising motorists. Most calculations of whether motorists are paying all the costs they incur simply try to balance construction and main-tenance cost of roads with income from fuel taxes, registration fees and tolls. This simplistic formula ignores the following costs:

■ *The income-earning potential of the land held out of use by roads or road reserves.* Ian Manning argues that:

> No private business is content that its current revenue should equal expenditure; it wants a return on its capital as well... In urban areas approximately 80 per cent of the capital value of the road system lies in the value of the land. As a rough calculation, sufficient only to give an order of magnitude, if the motorists of Sydney were required to pay a 15 per cent dividend on the value of the metropolitan road system the cost of motoring in cents per kilometre would approximately double.[25]

One could also argue that the motorists should not only have to pay a rent at current commercial rates for the land occupied by roads; they should also pay the council rates as if the land were occupied by a building.

■ *The infrastructure costs of urban sprawl.* Increasing road infrastruc-ture feeds urban sprawl which forces a greater per capita cost for provision and maintenance of water, electricity, gas, sewerage, drainage, and even more roads.

- *Loss in agricultural productivity.* Urban sprawl often eats into the most fertile farming areas forcing farming of less productive land and/or the transporting of produce over greater distances, forcing up prices.

- Public transport deficit. The public transport deficit really belongs to the car drivers. Before cars replaced public transport as the chief means of transport, most public transport companies or departments ran at a profit. Even in the US, public transport companies once ran at a profit – $60 million in 1960. Between 1940 and 1948, Seattle Transit System farebox profits were over $12 million.[26] In 1939 Los Angeles Railway Corporation paid taxes of nearly $1 million and still made an operating profit of approximately $750,000. In total, about $175 million was paid to government bodies by Chicago transit companies from 1907 to 1931.[27] Not only did they run at a profit and pay taxes, they also paid for all street maintenance and even paid to have the streets swept. By 1975, the US public transport deficit stood at $400 million.[28]

  Current losses are therefore caused by the motorist's decision to use their own private form of transport rather than that provided by the community for everyone's benefit. One could argue that the only socially responsible thing for a motorist to do is pay the community a fee equivalent to what it would cost them to make each journey by public transport, this fee being used to maintain the public transport network at the same level of service and efficiency which would be possible if they did make that trip by public transport. It seems more than reasonable to apply this principle to at least the commuting trip which, in the big Australian cities in 1971, accounted for one-third of all the journeys in cities and half the total kilometres travelled.[29] Manning argues that:

  > According to the most conservative tradition in economics, an economic change is only unambiguously worthwhile if it makes some people better off without worsening the position of any others. If a change is made which contravenes this principle, those whose position is worsened may justly claim that they are bearing some of the costs of those whose position is improved and may therefore claim compensation from them.[30]

- *Costs of deaths and injuries.* Private motor vehicles impose a much higher death and accident rate than public transport. These costs, which are imposed by the motoring community, should be born by the motoring community – not by the non-motoring community. According to an Australian Bureau of Transport and Communications

Economics Study in 1989, road accidents cost the community $6.2 billion dollars – $382 for every man, woman and child. If car owners were to pay their share of death and accident costs, it would cost each of them an extra $673 per year.

- *Car parks.* Car parks eat up valuable land that could be used for exchange opportunities. They are also costly to build and maintain. These costs are usually passed on to customers in the price of the services or goods provided. Thus a motorist who drives to a regional shopping centre pays part of the cost of their car park in the goods they buy. But the other part is paid by the people who arrived on foot, by bike or by public transport. This is a direct cross-subsidisation.

- Pollution. Cars are one of the major contributors to greenhouse gases, smog and acid rain. Everyone pays for the damage caused.

- Congestion. One car too many on a road can trigger congestion. This not only causes massive time delays for tens of thousands of people, but it also delays public transport and makes commerce less efficient. These increased transport costs must be passed on to consumers in the price of their goods and services, regardless of whether they were part of the cause of the congestion or not.

Todd Litman documents 14 of these external costs which motorists do not currently pay and which are borne by society in general. His estimates (1991) were that in the US, motorists would need to pay an extra 47.1 cents per passenger mile in peak periods and 30.1 cents per passenger mile out of peak times if they were to bear the true costs of their motoring.[31]

Right to a nurturing environment

All people have a right to the urban environment that best encourages social, spiritual, intellectual, cultural, emotional and physical well-being and helps individuals develop to their full potential.

In practice this means a right to have:

- interaction with family, friends and acquaintances protected from restrictions imposed artificially by traffic;

- social interaction, recreational activities and sleep protected from excessive noise intrusion;

- full use of home and yard – not subjugated by noise intrusion;

- clean air free from pollutants which may pose health problems.

Children's rights to independent safe passage to school, play space for interaction with friends and other facilities essential for their development must also be protected. Children also have the right to explore their neighbourhood in safety in ever increasing circles as they mature and to be unimpeded in developing a relationship with their neighbourhood. These rights must be couched both negatively and positively. Society has a duty to create a positive environment which encourages individuals to flourish and reach their full potential. This implies encouraging an interactive neighbourhood where individuals can make their unique contributions whether of a cultural, relational, material, intellectual, social or spiritual nature. Expressed from the negative perspective, this right advocates the removal of those elements which stop the neighbourhood and the individual reaching their full potential, elements such as noise, pollution or rivers of traffic which cut people off from one another.

Right to street space
All people have first priority to use of the living space (street) in front of their homes with rights for others to use that space decreasing in proportion to the distance they live from the street space. Responsibility to act as a guest while using a street increases in proportion to the distance a person lives from the space.

A German Ministry for Regional and Urban Planning publication in 1979 noted: 'Your home street must become like a living room...'.[32] And again, in 1982: 'The streets of tomorrow make traffic more bearable by creating a home environment in the street. The streets will belong to the people and be part of their homes'.[33] The Dutch call their traffic calmed streets *woonerf* meaning 'living yard'. Many European cities are attempting to recover the centuries old tradition of seeing the street as part of people's living space.

Jan Tanghe in *Living Cities* recognises this century old tradition when he talks of the fundamental choice facing our cities.

> The crucial question to be put here is whether or not the city, which was formerly built on the human scale, and in which the street existed primarily as a means of contact, is to be replaced by a megapolis where the dimensions of the street are on the scale required for its primary use by mechanical transport...

> The urban environment should again become a place favourable for human encounter; for looking around, listening and talking to people, walking about and sitting down. Streets and squares should once again be treated as outside rooms within the city, as places where the opportunity of contact between people is the primary consideration.[34]

Recognising that streets are living space and an extension of people's living room raises a peculiar ownership problem. Who owns the street? Streets are not the exclusive private property of those fronting them. Nor are they owned equally by the whole city like the town hall, city square, community playing fields or public highway. Ownership falls somewhere between total private and total public ownership. The street space in front of a particular house belongs primarily to those residents, but not exclusively. It also belongs to those living two doors away, but not to the same degree. It also belongs to the person on the other side of town, but with a greatly diminished level of ownership. So 'ownership' of street space diminishes in proportion to the distance a person lives from it and responsibility to act as a guest increases in proportion to the distance people live from it.

This is an important concept in the rights battle. At the moment there is an unspoken assumption that the streets of the city belong equally to everyone and therefore there is a divine right for people to drive where they want to, when they want to.

This concept of ownership raises a complex question. How does society view the ownership of roads designed for mass movement of vehicles such as arterials; particularly when people's houses front these roads? Firstly, from an idealistic and theoretical point of view, it is possible to view a city as having two types of carriageways; streets where local people live which are owned primarily by local people and public highways for the movement of pedestrians, cyclists and motorised vehicles (if permitted) which are owned equally by the entire community as a public asset.

In reality, what has happened in many cities is that residential streets have been turned into public highways and called arterials, sub-arterials or collectors. In this case one would have to argue that morally these streets still belong primarily to the people who live there and hard decisions such as banning cars for commuting, except in exceptional circumstances, may have to be taken to protect the rights of those residents. While this may seem impossible in the curent political climate, one can draw some hope from the successes of the anti-smoking lobby.

Right to extra vigilance
All vulnerable people have a right to extra vigilance from the community to protect all the above rights on their behalf.

And here I have come the full circle again, for it is impossible to have an interactive community if the vulnerable and easily marginalised, who have an invaluable contribution to make, have been locked out of participation. Locking these people out not only erodes their rights but ours also. In fact our survival and the survival of the planet may depend upon enactment of this very right.

5

Rebuilding the Eco-City together

I'll pay you well
If you will tell
Where I do dwell
And take me home.
Old street song

We must look beyond the car into the artificial heart of
modern society if we are to save ourselves from an
object that is but a projection of our own unsatisfied
desires.
Jeremiah Creedon[1]

Today it is prosperity that is externally ugly...we sit
starving amidst our gold, the Midas of the Ages.
William Morris, *Forecasts of the*
Coming Century, 1897[2]

The future of mankind will ultimately be decided by
the choice between the city, which contains the seeds of
man's salvation, and the machine which, as a
substitute for happiness, may eventually be the cause of
his complete destruction...
Jan Tanghe[3]

Trend is not destiny.
Lewis Mumford[4]

Metamorphosis and the machine – people calming

Without detracting from all that has been said about traffic-induced human rights abuses, these abuses are not due primarily to the number or nature of cars and trucks. Cars do not drive themselves. The root cause of these human rights abuses is the way we view the city, the world and ourselves. The solution is ultimately not legislation but a change of attitude. Although declaration of a *Bill of Access-to-Exchange Rights* may be an important step in the educative process, two fundamental shifts of perception are needed: attitude to the city and attitude to ourselves.

Ebenezer Howard reacted to the overcrowded and dehumanising conditions of industrial London by proposing his Garden City. But there is an ironic twist to Howard's solution; he unwittingly perpetuated the very problem he sought to solve by adopting a solution which was essentially mechanistic in nature.

Whatever Howard's internal beliefs or motivations, his Garden City solution left his disciples with the belief that the city's ills could be fixed by an authoritarian imposition of harmony and order. Making the city a better machine would make better people. The town planning movement, to which he gave birth, failed to make a transition which would have seen the city as an organism, an eco-system, with its own internal life, creative energy and interdependence. Howard failed to understand that the fundamental problem with the industrial city was the philosophi-

cal outlook of its inhabitants; they had sold their souls and their humanness for the output of a machine.

The town planning movement, by and large, still views the city as a machine. Decisions on road networks are based on a notion of efficiency which is being measured in the quantifiables of dollars, seconds and kilometres per hour, not in how well the city encourages or discourages creative relationships between people. When efficiency is measured in terms of output of the machine, it makes sense to widen a road in order to move more cars per hour.

Ethos – not techniques

In planning cities so they promote a rich diversity of exchange, it is not new techniques for fine-tuning the machine that are necessary, but a whole new ethos – a new way of looking at cities and the people that inhabit them. Viewing the city as a machine for economic production will always lead to dehumanising of the inhabitants.

To focus on techniques is to put the cart before the horse. Regardless of how good a particular technique looks, or the spirit in which the technique is promoted, it will become corrupted if the underlying assumptions and view of the city has not changed. If the city is still viewed as a machine, the focus of the new technique will become efficiency rather than neighbourhood life. Certainly a new ethos will carry with it new techniques, but the ethos must be the centre of attention, not the techniques.

Poor self-image too often leads to self-destruction. And nothing leads to poor self-image more quickly than to see oneself as nothing more than a machine. If we cling to a mechanistic view of life, no amount of fiddling with structures will change the way we relate to the city and, in the end, how we relate to each other. On the other hand, if we view the city as an interactive people's place – a place for living, a place for relationships – then the creative drive within us will modify the existing structure. The change must first come in our internal view of the city.

People calming

CART experienced first-hand how a vision can become corrupted if the underlying values and the world view that prompt the vision are not first carefully laid out. Initially, an attempt was made by some planning professionals to discredit traffic calming. But within two years of its release many planners in Australia had adopted some of the techniques of Traffic Calming, and in many cases even the rhetoric. Unfortunately, most also clung to the old planning ethos which sees the city and its streets as a machine rather than a people's place. The result has been a continuation of auto-dominant planning sprinkled with traffic calming techniques and sometimes a dab of traffic calming rhetoric on top to make the old recipe more palatable.

One person who saw very early the revolutionary nature of what CART was advocating was Phil Day, one of Brisbane's most senior and respected town planners. In his review of Traffic Calming he said:

> Traffic Calming involves a fundamental re-thinking of metropolitan planning and organisation – and a revived emphasis upon quality rather than quantity of life. Some may even see the ultimate goal as the calming of society itself – an abandonment of the frenetic pursuit of ever more development and the increasing inequalities it is generating, and an eschewing of the ever-increasing consumption of the finite resources of a fragile planet.[5]

Day's comments take us to the very heart of the problem. When people lose sight of themselves as intricate parts of an eco-system (part of an interactive community) and see themselves as machines, then they start to measure their self-worth in mechanical terms; efficiency, production, speed and power. Life becomes the pursuit of techniques and technologies that will improve their machine qualities.

Herein lies the deep psychological significance of the automobile. The driver slips behind the wheel and is assimilated into the machine, becoming one with it. The machine becomes an extension of the driver's 'machineness', promising to enhance power, speed, efficiency and productivity. Metamorphosis takes place as the driver is transformed from homo-sapiens to homo-machine; both hearts of steel united in their drive for efficiency, speed and power. The driver becomes the driven.

Am I exaggerating this transformation? Stand and watch pedestrians some day. Do they wear horns to honk at each other? Jostle each other? Cut each other off? Make rude gestures at each other? If five seconds is unimportant when walking, why does half a second become a matter of life and death when driving? Maybe the car is like a bottle of booze in that it strips away the veneer and exposes the real self – in this case revealing someone in a quest for efficiency, production, speed and power. On the other hand, walking may quell the demon spirit within us, and like the sun opening the flower, encourage our suppressed humanness to show itself.

There is no doubt that the car puts enormous power in one person's hands. Suddenly people can dominate time and space, at least that is the illusion. Their 'zone-of-influence' is dramatically increased. When people walk, they stand on equal terms with the rest of humanity. Their zone-of-influence is the distance over which messages can be read in another person's eyes, probably a maximum of 15 metres. But when they are behind the wheel of the car, they are suddenly given the power to intimidate others from a distance of 150 metres, a massive increase in their zone-of-influence. Many people have this internal desire for power and control and it is this desire that the car taps.

> [The steam engine's] great significance was pointed out by Matthew Bolton who had joined in partnership with James Watt to manufacture the engine. When James Boswell, the biographer, came to see Bolton in his factory in 1776, he told him: 'I sell here, sir, what all the world desires to have: power'.[6]

Add to this the power of anonymity. It is very easy to treat someone as a non-human when they are unknown to us. It becomes increasingly hard to exploit them as we form relationships and exchange parts of our humanness. The soldier who looks in the wallet of an enemy soldier he has just killed and finds a photo of his family will find it much harder to pull the trigger next time. Anonymity is the power base of the war machine. It is also that which allows us to intimidate children and people with walking-sticks at pedestrian crossings, or steal their play space and home territory.

Then there is the power of 'imputed persona'. The car manufacturers, in league with their advertising agencies, invent a persona which a particular vehicle imparts to the owner: the wild adventurer; the independent career woman; the knight who always rescues his maiden; the high-powered executive. These people are going places, so stand aside.

And perhaps underlying all of the above is the modern, materialistic outlook with its pressure to succeed, as the following newspaper story demonstrates:

> From now on, I am refusing to go anywhere on Monday mornings – not even the corner store. This is when motivated sales people unleash themselves on the highway, raring to sell, sell, sell. Some, doubtless, will succeed. Others, excited beyond endurance by the sales director's Monday morning pep talks, simply hurtle their cars into less motivated road-users. Positive thinking has turned them into lethal weapons – a case of 'buy, sucker, or I'll mow you down'.

> The phenomenon came to light when an insurance company noted that one of its corporate clients was experiencing accidents every Monday at 11.30am. They investigated and traced the problem to the firm's motivational sessions. Presumably the sales director has modified his pitch to a few notches below psychopathic desperation. But there is another possibility. The company may have invested in a fleet of armored cars – just to make a proper job of it.[7]

The new eco-relational planning ethos for our cities has at its heart people calming. It assumes a dramatic shift in our values away from enslavement to the twin deities of the machine age: automobile and clock. Away from efficiency, production, speed and power. It embraces the elements that make us truly human and recognises that these elements refuse to be dictated to by time. Friendships, creativity, inspiration, revelation and wisdom live in a timeless world and make their appearance on the stage when their seasons come. They rebel and flee when bustled. They know nothing of efficiency, speed, power or the work ethic. They only bring their gifts to those who live by seasons, not by seconds.

Do cities make the people – or vice versa?

So far I have skirted a crucial question. To what extent does the city environment affect the quality of life which people can live?

It is interesting to compare writers' perceptions of what makes the perfect city setting and what to them would be 'hell'. For Hugh Stretton, the suburbs are heaven and high-density city living would be hell.

> Less compassionate critics depict dreary dormitories where life shrivels, festers, taps its foot in family prisons…conversations, if any, are boring; neighbours pry. Mum does the dishes, dad potters and mows, the kids pick their acne between homework and the telly.

> Suburb-haters, thinking of people without personal resources in ill-designed houses and gardens, too often undervalue the free and satisfying self-expression, the mixture of community and privacy, fond familiarity and quick change and escape, which this minuscule subdivision and diversification of the quarter-acre's spaces can offer to the lives it houses. Compared with it, the private realm of the city apartment is internally monotonous, and its owners more restricted in what he can make of it. He loses a whole field for self-expression, and many chances to adapt his environment to idiosyncratic needs. He has only one escape. That one may be into the crowded city's full and valuable diversity, but he can't go there undressed. That escape is to nowhere quiet or private, to nothing he can kick, dig up, re-plan, encourage to grow, or hang a wet shirt on. In many cities the landless apartment is where the rich get most neuroses and the poor get most delinquents.[8]

The 'suburb hater' to whom Stretton refers could well have been the New York journalist Michelle Landsberg who takes the opposite point of view.

> Straight out the door – no front yard or walk or dreary evergreen shrubs to distance me – I am in the thick of city life. Within two blocks of my apartment building I can get my clothes cleaned, pick up hot brioches for breakfast from a French baker, sit in an airy cafe for an espresso, post a letter, buy disks for my computer, dawdle through great museums and dozens of private art galleries, stock up on bagels and lox, pick up grapefruit spoons or teenagers' socks at ritzy Bloomingdale's or dirt-cheap Alexander's, or choose among three different supermarkets…ur-banologists have deplored New York's chaotic squalor but to me it is a

better place to live than to visit.[9]

So who is right? In one sense both. As Stretton so rightly goes on to say:

> ...minds can be parched in any sort of urban fabric – or nourished in almost any... Plenty of dreary lives are indeed lived in suburbs... Intelligent critics don't blame the suburbs for the empty aspirations: the aspirations are what corrupt the suburbs. The car is washed on Sunday mornings because its owner has been brought up to think of nothing better to do, not because suburbs prohibit better thought.[10]

The apparent truth of this struck home to me one day as I sat on a huge, rocky outcrop. There, growing in the slightest crack was a small tree. I was captivated. How on earth could this tree survive in such a hostile place? I was struck by the tree's stark beauty; twisted limbs and gnarled exposed roots. The story of every storm seemed to be reflected in its form. Its beauty emanated from its persistent will to live against the greatest odds.

As I sat there I saw the faces of people I knew reflected in the tree – people who had also survived in a hostile environment. An adult who as a child was the victim of horrific child abuse. Another person anchored to a wheelchair, racked with constant pain. The eternal battler who seems to have been buffeted by one storm after another; death of parents as a child, movement from foster home to foster home, loss of partner, etc. These survivors also exude an inner beauty which causes us to marvel, a beauty which comes from their persistent will to live against the greatest odds. Not only to live, but a determination to turn the hostile elements into a source of life and strength. It is this same sense of purpose, this determination to live and shape their future, which causes people in concentration camps to turn a place of torture into a home.

Does this mean then that people should purposely create cities which are hostile and oppressive? Should they build concentration camps so they can marvel and be inspired by the way the human spirit can conquer the most hostile environment and triumph? The answer is obviously no. For the wonder of the tree on the rocky outcrop or on the desert plain is that it has survived at all. Part of its beauty is that it stands defiantly alone. Thousands of other trees tried to grow and died. For every adult who has endured child abuse and converted it into a positive life-force, there are many more who have been destroyed. For every person who has turned the horrors of a concentration camp into ennobled life, there are thousands who were crushed and perished.

By comparison, a rainforest is also a place of beauty and life. Like the tree on the rocky outcrop, it also converts death forces into life. As leaves fall from the trees and die, as plants and animals themselves die, their death is recycled into life. But unlike the rocky outcrop, here life and spontaneity are encouraged. Here diversity flourishes and reaches new dimensions.

This is the vision of the Eco-City. It is to create a living environment which gives life to those who would have perished on the rocky outcrop. It is also to create an environment in which those who have survived on the outcrop can find comfort and support – an environment in which their pain can be recycled into life for others. Certain structural arrangements either promote this kind of interactive community or retard it. While Hugh Stretton may well have made a home in the desert of his dormitory suburb, one suspects he would discover an even more enriching life in a city designed as an Eco-City.

Five clues from nature

It is time to start drawing together the threads running through the previous chapters into courses of practical action which will help evolve a city form which will take humanity to the next stage of the evolutionary process. By looking at the nature of organisms and eco-systems we can discern five essential characteristics of the Eco-City.

Inner form and balance
All organisms have inner form – cells, tissue and organs – which interact and are organised in a way that maximises the efficiency of each part and allows each part to make its vital contribution to the life of the organism. These parts must not only be in their rightful place, they must also be kept in balance. If one leg of the athlete is six inches shorter than the other, balance between the various organs is destroyed and overall efficiency dramatically reduced. Turning too much living space into road space destroys the inner form and balance of the city. Such things as neighbourhood stores, even small things such as chairs, art, fountains, and safe walkways, play an essential part in the inner form and balance.

Internal efficiency
The parts of a body or organism are related in a way which enables maximum output for minimum effort. Unnecessary bulk usually leads to inefficiency.

To achieve this efficiency nature uses fractal systems. Earlier I illustrated the nature of fractal systems by describing a painting within a painting within a painting. A tree is also fractal – a seemingly chaotic branching arrangement, yet with its own internal order. A characteristic of fractal systems is that they are in microcosm what they are in macrocosm. In other words, break a branch from a tree, put the broken

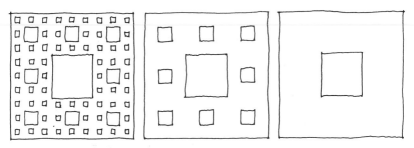

Fig. 11: Two-dimensional fractal design.

end in the ground and it looks like a tree. The same chaotic yet ordered system of branching is there. Break off a section of the branch and it too looks like a miniature tree. Even a small twig can look like a miniature tree. What is seen then, when looking at a tree, is a tree within a tree within a tree within a tree.

Fractal systems are not hierarchical. A tree does not go from trunk to major branches to minor branches to twigs to leaves. These are convenient labels for reductionist thinkers who want to reduce things to their base building blocks and draw hierarchical flow charts. In nature it just does not work that way. Growing on the trunk of the tree you will find minor branches or twigs or even leaves – with no intervening stages. In many plants, any part of the plant is capable of becoming the whole plant. Plant the branch and you get a complete tree. The words 'trunk' or 'branch' or 'twig' are only useful as a means of indicating at what scale the tree is being viewed. 'Trunk' indicates the tree is being viewed in a macro sense. 'Branch' indicates the tree is being viewed within the tree. 'Twig' indicates the tree is being viewed within the tree within the tree.

At present, planners are locked into fairly simplistic hierarchical models: city centre, regional centre, suburban centre, neighbourhood centre, home; freeway, arterial, sub-arterial, collector, residential street. But the neighbourhood is a city within the city. The word 'neighbourhood' is just a convenient label to describe at what scale we are viewing the city.

Fractal systems are incredibly efficient because they carry within them the possibility of infinite surface in a finite space. Imagine taking a carpet square and dividing it into nine equal squares then removing the middle square (fig. 11). Then take the eight remaining squares and repeat the process for each one; divide into nine equal squares and remove the middle one. Then repeat the process again. You are creating a fractal design. Now imagine repeating a similar process in three dimensions on a cube (fig. 12). Theoretically it is possible to continue removing material from the cube forever. The total surface area of the resultant sponge

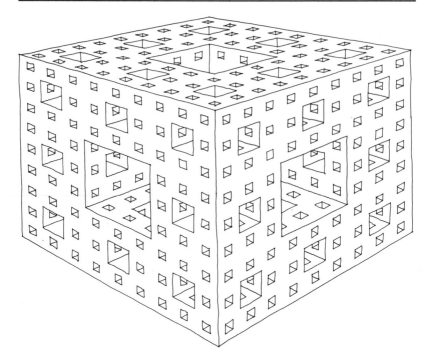

Fig. 12: Three-dimensional fractal design (Menger sponge).

(called a Menger sponge) would be infinite; infinite surface area in a finite space.

The hierarchical view has led to zoning that divides the city into segregated parts which are single purpose (for example, industry, or commerce, or flats, or family homes). While this segregation does not inhibit same-type exchanges (industry to industry, commerce to commerce), it does inhibit diversity of exchange. This is because the surface area for exchange, or the interfaces between these functions, is greatly diminished by zoning. If every street, every neighbourhood becomes the city in microcosm, reflecting the full diversity of the city, then a richer range of exchange is facilitated. In fact, the more segregated a city, the less space is available for exchange. A fractal view, however, which sees a city within a city within a city, carries with it the possibilities of the Menger sponge – 'infinite' area for exchange, a secret tapped already by the human lungs and blood system.

Many body systems are fractal. Earlier I showed how efficient such a system can be with the blood system being able to deliver blood to within two or three cells yet only taking up five per cent of body space. The lungs provide an exchange surface the size of a tennis court, interlaced with blood vessels to collect oxygen.

Internal unity

The parts of a body are united in their purpose – to live and create new order and life-forms out of chaos. What is chronically lacking in many cities (particularly those in Australia and the United States) is a 'city ethos' that gives cities cohesion. As Kenneth Schneider so rightfully observes: 'Great cities will not be built until Americans decide to write the city into the American Dream'.[11]

Micro-level health

What we learn from organisms and eco-systems is that the health of individual parts or cells is of fundamental importance to the health of the body corporate. Cancerous cells can be fatal. Extinction of one micro-organism in a rainforest may upset the delicate balance and eventually destroy it. Functioning neighbourhoods are the 'cells' of the Eco-City. Therefore a priority in building a healthy city must be building healthy neighbourhoods.

External balance

Each organism or eco-system is part of a larger eco-system. The city must be seen as part of the world eco-system and must be carefully interfaced with the natural environment.

Ten guidelines for re-building the Eco-City

Build healthy neighbourhoods

The goal here is to promote micro-level health.

- *Define neighbourhood*

  It is extremely hard to start building up the health of neighbourhoods if they have no boundaries. Defining boundaries does not mean building fences or drawing red lines on a map. It is an art which must take into account natural landscape features, existing structure of the built environment and the other factors below.

- *Define the neighbourhood hub*

  Each neighbourhood must have its own internal life. It therefore will need its own vibrant hub which will usually be a gathering of shops, other community facilities, local government offices and a transit centre. Before any new residential development takes place, the boundaries of the neighbourhood/s and their centre/s must be clearly defined.

■ *Enrich defined neighbourhoods as complete urban growth units*
Each neighbourhood should become as self-sufficient as possible. In fact, this will become the future art of city building; integration of living, shopping, recreation, social interaction, work, and cultural activities into compact neighbourhoods to avoid forced travel. These enriched neighbourhoods, according to Schneider:

> should function close enough to the individual to respond directly to them as a person, to give them a sense of power in determining their course of life, and to encourage them to be a vital participant in society. Community should provide a sense of place, a social context, and a personal continuity necessary for a personal integrity in society. The current massive, undifferentiated form of the city demands large, specialised programs that do not suit people and that leave them powerless and frustrated.[12]

These neighbourhood growth centres should contain the administration centre for local government affairs. They should produce as much of the goods and services consumed by the neighbourhood as possible (including food) and allow the local recycling of waste. They should provide for social interaction and stimulate the growth of individuals through provision of amenities, encouraging cultural growth through providing opportunities for self-expression. They should have a character that is recognised and celebrated, and they should rationalise movement of people and goods by having a strong focal point.

■ *Maximise internal efficiency of each neighbourhood*
Creation of these strong neighbourhood centres will start to rationalise the movement of people and goods. Instead of requiring four trips to diverse destinations, a number of tasks can be accomplished by one trip to a central location. Trip distances are reduced, thereby allowing a greater proportion of trips to be made by foot or cycle or, alternatively, by community-based public transport such as an electric mini-bus. In practical terms this means constructing or providing safe walk- and cycle-ways that lead to the neighbourhood hub. The goal should be that every person, if physically capable, will be able to reach the neighbourhood hub by foot or cycle, in safety and without being discouraged by conflict with motorised traffic.

■ *Build identity*
Many of the measures outlined above will begin to build neighbourhood identity. Another way may be to record and publish the oral history of a neighbourhood. This may take the form of a 'recollections board' where people could pin up stories about interesting things they remember or display photographs. Someone may be responsible for collecting copies of all this material and changing the display on a regular basis. It could also take the form of a yarn night where a writer collates the stories and they are retold by local actors. People can develop a sense of placeness about their neighbourhood only if they are aware of its history.

Ways must also be found to encourage children to explore their neighbourhood and to develop a relationship with its features. They could be encouraged to develop a map which shows all the interesting places in their neighbourhood and the safest routes for getting to them. They could also be encouraged to have an input into the evolution of their neighbourhood.

■ *Build a strong street life*
I have tried to stress the importance of seeing the neighbourhood as a city within the city, as a part of the fractal system I wrote of earlier. It is the branch which, when looked at in isolation, looks like a small version of the tree of which it is a part.

Looking at the neighbourhood, it is possible to see this same fractal dimension – neighbourhoods within neighbourhoods. Reference to 'street life' is an indication that we have dropped down another scale or increased the magnification. This smaller scale may involve the houses facing a street for one or two blocks. It may be a pocket of houses comprising a number of streets. Even at this level, planners should be trying to create the city within the city within the city. Many of the measures already outlined for the neighbourhood can be applied at this smaller scale: create a street focus; enrich community life of the street; maximise internal efficiency (e.g. mid-block walkways); build identity.

Strengthen the city centre

There are many specialised facilities and services which cannot be provided in neighbourhood centres. These should be located in the city centre for the obvious reason of rationalising access to these facilities. The city centre should be seen as containing the 'specialist organs' of the body. These should not be located on the outside fringe of the body, but internally and centrally. It is here that the cultural experiences that take place in microcosm at the neighbourhood level happen on a grander scale. The focus of the city centre must be people, diverse cultural expression, commerce and colourful exchange.

There is debate among planners about whether cities should centralise or decentralise. There is a third alternative: a fractal 're-centralising' of the city at all scales. For example, a city may be large enough to support four universities so these would be decentralised to a regional level but centralised within each region; it may be large enough to support 40 specialist shops of a certain kind and these would be decentralised to a district level but centralised within each district – and so on right down to the street level. The principle is to bring the exchange opportunity as close as possible to the maximum number of people.

To those who argue that a vibrant social and cultural life cannot be sustained simultaneously at the neighbourhood level and city centre I would reply that they do not yet understand the dynamics of the Eco-City. Each section of the human body has its own internal life and structure yet participates in a wider life. If a finger is hit hard with a hammer, the whole body suffers. The health of the whole is dependent on the health of the individual parts and the health of the individual parts is dependent on the health of the rest of the body. It is from a healthy social and cultural life of neighbourhoods that we will find the creative energy and enthusiasm for a healthy social and cultural life at the city centre – and vice versa.

Optimise exchange efficiency

The goal of the Eco-City is to maximise exchange while minimising the costs (resources and time). In other words to *optimise exchange efficiency*. To understand this concept, imagine a bag of beans as 'currency' with which to buy access to exchange opportunities. In other words, it is possible to trade some of the beans for a car, a bike, shoes, a seat on public transport, a telephone, or a share in a home delivery vehicle. Beans must also be traded for the space occupied while travelling, for

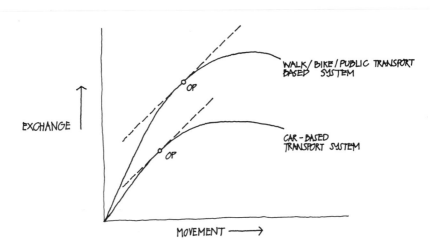

EXCHANGE

WALK/ BIKE / PUBLIC TRANSPORT
BASED SYSTEM

CAR - BASED
TRANSPORT SYSTEM

MOVEMENT ⟶

Fig. 13: Optimum Point (OP) of exchange efficiency for two types of transport systems.

storing a vehicle at the other end, for the fuel used (there is a large premium on non-renewable energy sources) and for time spent travelling. Besides, beans must be put up as surety against fouling the air with pollutants or noise and against the erosion of other people's exchange opportunities. The greater the fouling of the air or erosion of exchange opportunities, the lower the rebate.

Optimising exchange efficiency is receiving optimum exchange for the minimum number of beans. Looking at the exchange efficiency curve explored earlier in the book (fig. 13) we can see that there is an optimum point of exchange efficiency which changes according to how transport is arranged in the city. There are many ways of increasing exchange efficiency:

■ *Bring the destinations to the people*
   Instead of spending money on road space, time and resources to transport people to an exchange opportunity, spend the same amount on bringing the exchange opportunity closer to the home-base. This may take the form of home-deliveries, tele-commuting or enriching neighbourhood centres. While the initial investment may be the same (or even higher), the on-going cost decreases dramatically.

■ *Increase density of housing, job opportunities and exchange opportunities*
   Higher densities mean less distance to cover between exchange opportunities and greater potential to fulfil a number of tasks in one

129

trip. Spread an organism over too wide an area and you kill it. Cities are, by very definition, a concentration of people in a specific locality. Peter Newman and Jeffrey Kenworthy have amply demonstrated that density is one of the keys to building energy efficient cities and viable public transport systems. In their ground-breaking comparison study of 32 international cities, they showed that while European cities had living densities in outer areas four times higher than those in the United States, they consumed four times less gasoline per head.[13] The study concludes that if cities are to have their gasoline and automobile dependence lowered then land-use intensity (number of people, jobs and facilities per hectare) has to be increased.[14]

In Australia, the United States and to a lesser degree Britain, there is a deep seated aversion to the concept of higher density living. It conjures up images of high-rise apartment slums. Anyone who has experienced the low-rise, high-density living of some European cities will know that these fears are based on a wide range of myths.

For example I stayed in a row house in Bayreuth. The home had as much internal space as my Australian home. But instead of this space being spread horizontally over a large area, it had been creatively arranged in a vertical pattern. At the back was a small private courtyard where we could sip coffee and yarn. At the front was a huge commons, a park shared by all the other row houses, where there was play equipment, seats and a table-tennis table. The feeling of space is much greater in European cities than it is in Australia where public space is divided up into private quarter-acre blocks. These large

blocks can create the same intimate spaces as the Bayreuth courtyard, but they can never match the practicality or spaciousness of the commons. Yet arrangements like the row house allow five times the number of people to live in the same area, including their commons.

It is my belief that density paranoia is on the decline in Australia. In any case I believe it will largely take care of itself as people are integrated into neighbourhoods which are bursting with social and cultural life. It will be a fact of life that people in those communities with the highest densities, together with integrated mixed zoning, will tend to have the most diverse and interesting lifestyles. Other neighbourhoods will want the same.

■ *Creatively mix housing, job opportunities and exchange opportunities*
I showed earlier that the more fractal the city becomes the more area becomes available for exchange. The current practice of zoning sections of the city for industry, others for housing, others for commerce, gives the city a coarse 'mixed-use' grain. The larger and coarser this grain, the more travel is required and the less area there is available for exchange.

Other strategies for optimising exchange efficiency include: using means of transport that are 'exchange-friendly'; encouraging the mixed use of streets for both movement and exchange; giving first priority to transport that uses renewable energy resources and second priority to those that use non-renewable resources with the greatest efficiency; optimising the number of people using each vehicle; encouraging 'trip chaining' – saving less important trips up and combining them into one journey; reducing cross-commuting.

Whilst pro-active policies can be designed to accomplish each of these, all other planning decisions must be tested with the question: 'Will this help optimise exchange efficiency or decrease it?' It is hard to imagine any decision that a local, state or federal authority makes that does not have some impact on exchange efficiency.

This will necessitate governments developing mechanisms for taking account of the external costs of decisions. Because of increasing trends to 'corporatisation' of government departments, they tend to make decisions that will increase internal efficiency but which externalise the costs onto the community or other departments. For example, education departments close down small schools and amalgamate them into a larger facility because it is cheaper for them, but then the community pays for this 'efficiency' at the petrol bowser and in their rates. Or the road department is required to build a bigger road to cope with the increased traffic. These mechanisms must make plain to politicians those instances where, in the long run, it will be cheaper and more efficient to put funds into keeping the school open than having to fund a road widening in 12 months time.

Charge the true costs for access to exchange opportunities

While I used beans to illustrate the concept of exchange efficiency, a similar system must be devised which reflects the true cost of giving access to exchange opportunities if we are to create the most efficient Eco-City possible. Currently those who use inefficient means of reaching their exchange opportunities are rewarded. For example, I explained earlier how those walking, cycling or using public transport subsidise the parking costs of the person who drives. This is taking money from the pockets of those acting in the best interests of the city and giving it to those who are not! Motorists then ask who is it that will fund the public transport deficit. The answer is simple. There would not be a deficit if those using private cars used the publicly provided means. It may be countered that the car drivers are paying for the deficit in their taxes, but so are those who are dependent on public transport. Even if the car drivers were picking up the total public transport deficit, they still would not be paying for the services that would exist if the motorists were still using the public transport system. Again, the person dependent on public transport is asked to carry this cost in increased travel times, inconvenience, or, in many cases, inability to travel at all.

A more equitable arrangement would be if car drivers paid an equivalent public transport fee for each journey they make in a car. This is the only way in which the public transport system can be maintained at the same level of operation and profitability it would have had if private car drivers were using the publicly provided means.

This guideline calls for authorities and the community to ask if the true costs of providing access are reflected in a policy decision. This does not necessarily mean that these costs will be extracted in the form of money. A city may decide that the 'cost' of providing access to the city centre during peak times for private petrol-driven vehicles is so high that it will put a ban on such vehicles entering during certain hours. Or it may only allow those with four occupants to enter during these times. Alternatively it may offer positive incentives such as the building of 'green' bridges (bridges that can only be used by pedestrians and cyclists – not cars) to shorten the distance exchange-friendly modes have to travel compared to car traffic.

While this guideline advocates a 'user pays' policy (reflecting *all* costs), society may choose to pay some or all of these costs for those easily marginalised because it recognises the benefits of having these people participate actively in the life of the city. This must never be viewed as a subsidy, which would be paternalistic and demeaning, but it is a price society pays for a service – the invaluable contribution these people bring to the Eco-City.

Promote the 'exchange-friendly' modes of transport

There are many ways of promoting the exchange-friendly modes of transport.

- Increase the safety of walk- and cycle-ways.

- Make walking and cycling more pleasant by incorporating drinking fountains, shade, shelter, seats, landscaping, artworks (sculptures, murals, pavement designs), market stalls, activity spots (outdoor chess, exercise equipment, play equipment for children), historical plaques, community information boards, or street performers.

- Interconnect the green modes. Give walk- and cycle-ways leading to public transport pick-up points priority over car traffic.

- Shorten the distance green modes have to go compared to the motor traffic.

Again, this guideline requires both the pro-active measures above and the modification of policies or plans which do not encourage a shift to green modes.

Convert planned exchanges into home-based or spontaneous exchanges

This guideline calls for a city-wide stocktake of all exchanges that are being fulfilled by people making a planned trip (a trip made specifically to fulfil a particular need). Each one of these must then be examined to see if it is possible to convert this exchange into a spontaneous or home-based exchange.

For example, one class of trip would be parents driving their children to a sporting fixture. How many of these trips could be eliminated if we made 50 per cent of our residential streets safer and virtually car free? How many trips could be eliminated if we created pocket parks in neighbourhoods with safe walk- and cycle-ways to them? How many trips could be eliminated if neighbourhoods organised their own sporting activities in the local school grounds which are not used at weekends and during holidays?

Another example is work trips. How many could be eliminated if high-tech work stations were provided either in people's homes or at neighbourhood centres? Instead of driving to work, these people would be connected to head office by computer equipment. Some people may argue that tele-commuting would cut down on exchanges in the work place, but it could be the rebirth of neighbourhood interaction. This time it may also be men (instead of primarily women) who participate in the building of community life. Tele-commuting may lead to Bill, who works for a large accountancy firm, ducking next door to have morning tea with Tom, Joan and Freda who all work from home. Or if they all work at work-stations provided at the neighbourhood centre, they may meet under the shade of a tree to play chess in their lunch hour.

Encourage diversity and the expression of diversity

This too involves both pro-active measures and measures to make sure diversity is not removed or expression limited. Pro-active measures include encouraging community art, neighbourhood talent quests, places for buskers, soap boxes, etc.

Special efforts need to be made to tap the wisdom, insight and creative potential of those easily marginalised. Often community arts workers have developed special skills for this purpose. As with the Munich chairs, we must not be afraid of chaos.

Build the 'commons'

The commons is a concept that has almost been lost in Western cities. Sim Van der Ryan and Peter Calthorpe explain how cheap energy and the automobile not only disbursed urban life, they also greatly reduced the shared domains – from courtyards, porticoes, and arcades to semiprivate streets, common yards and neighbourhood stores.

As a result, our public space lacks identity and is largely anonymous, while our private space strains towards a narcissistic autonomy. Our cities and communities are zoned black and white, private or public, my space or nobody's space... Inversely, private space is strained by the physical needs to provide for many activities which were once shared, and is further burdened by needs to create some identity in a surrounding sea of monotony.

With the new potential for unparalleled ownership and seemingly endless wealth, the private domain has quickly overtaken many of the functions of the public realm. Transportation moved from rail to car. Recreation moved from park to yard. Entertainment moved from circus to TV. Housing moved from townhouse to ranchette. Child care moved from neighbourhood and extended family to nuclear family. And commerce moved from the public street to private mall. The traditional balance and tension between public and private was overthrown, the middle ground was eliminated. The most intimate of the public domains were consumed by the private realm...

Sadly missing from the debate on the future of our cities is the notion of the commons; that the public domain must become richer as the private domain becomes more frugal; that the success and well-being must be a shared, rather than a private affair.[15]

The Neighbourhood Promenade Loop[16] (fig. 14) is just one measure that could help to rebuild the commons. This loop connects important activity centres in a neighbourhood: school, park, shopping centre, library, day-care centre, historical spots and transit stops. In runs on just one side of the road to save construction costs and to concentrate pedestrians. The promenade loop is fitted with seats, lighting for night safety, landscaping, sculptures, activity centres (exercise areas, outdoor chess boards, play equipment), plaques telling the history of long-term residents, community information boards, etc.

The Boulder Trail in Boulder, Colorado is a form of promenade loop. It connects a range of destinations – university, library, council head-quarters, hotel, high school, industrial estate. It has activity centres along its length – children's fishing ponds, exercise areas, sculpture gardens, underwater stream observatory, parks, educational displays, etc. For those who have walked the Boulder Trail, there is no doubt that it has become the social focus of the city. My host in Colorado complained that he would not use it on a Saturday or Sunday because 'it is worse than an LA freeway'. On a busy day, one in 20 Boulder residents will use the trail. I could not believe one of the signs along the trail: 'Beware. Congested Area Ahead'. Saturday is market day. People set up stalls along the edges of one of the parks and sell practically anything. In the

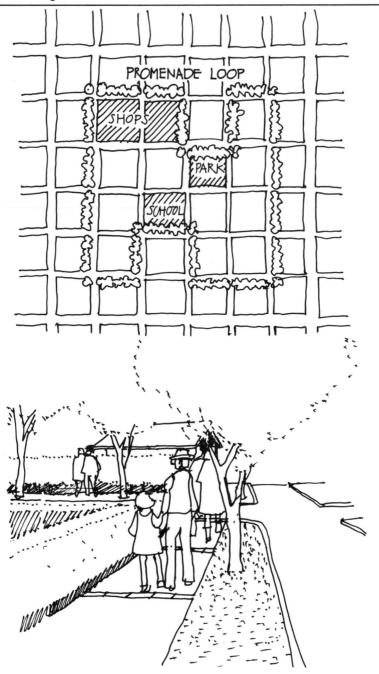

Fig. 14: Neighbourhood Promenade Loop

afternoon there is an outdoor concert at the hotel convention centre that backs onto the trail. An important part of the success of this trail is that it never crosses a road. For similar loops or trails to work, priority needs to be given to pedestrian traffic where the Loop crosses a road.

Give people and neighbourhoods greater control over decision making

In a previous chapter it was suggested that people should be encouraged to once again become 'generalists' and that they should be encouraged to bring their life experiences to bear on the decision making process.

Make those usually considered least, those considered most

From whichever philosophical viewpoint you design a city, this guideline should remain the one from which all others flow.

With every idea, with every decision, with every design, we must ask ourselves (or better still those usually marginalised from the decision-making process) what the impact of that idea, design, or decision will be on those usually considered least: children, those who are elderly, those who have 'disabilities', those who are 'poor', and those who cannot express themselves verbally. It is crucial to understand whether the impact of the design or policy will be to further marginalise these people or whether it will facilitate their greater participation in the life of the Eco-City.

This guideline brings a new meaning to the so called 'trickledown effect'. Traditionally this has been seen as follows: if you facilitate the increased well-being of those at the top of the heap (the rich and powerful), the benefits will trickle down to those below. This guideline turns the pyramid upside down. Those easily marginalised are at the top and the powerful are at the bottom, with the chief concern of the powerful being to serve those above them. In so doing, the benefits of facilitating the participation of the easily marginalised in city life trickles down to the rich and powerful. The rich and powerful discover new values, new perspectives on life. If there is no other motivation, self-interest demands society makes those easily marginalised as their chief consideration. While such a notion may sound idealistic and naïve in the extreme, its truth must be recognised and policies adopted which at least begin to encourage the easily marginalised to participate in the life of the city. These policies will include the encouragement of mixed socio-economic neighbourhoods and a priority on public transport, walking and cycling over private cars. It may be another one or two thousand years before the pyramid is inverted. But in the meantime, by changing our focus, we can start to create a dynamic, cosmopolitan city. Rich in its diversity. Seething with colour and life. Inspiring new heights of creativity. Prosperous beyond our wildest dreams.

No gain without pain? Rubbish!

I once spent time with the senior management of one of Australia's state road authorities. While they agreed that traffic was choking their city, the only solutions they could see involved restricting private car use. According to their assessment, the general public was not ready for the pain that would be necessary. They believed their political masters would not face reality because they did not want to be the bearers of the bad news. I challenged their assumption that there could be no gain without pain and we looked at a number of areas where there seemed to be great potential for relatively painless change.

Cross-commuting
The first area that I asked them to consider was cross-commuting. An 'efficient' road infrastructure encourages people to range wider for jobs. This leads to grossly inefficient cross-commuting with Tom and Freda working as service station attendants in each other's suburb and passing each other on the way to work. Ian Manning has calculated that in Melbourne and Sydney, two-thirds of people could find jobs within three or four kilometres of their homes if this was the overriding consideration in their job selection. Average work journey lengths in these cities, at the time of Manning's study, was 12 kilometres.[17] There is therefore great

potential gain if even just some of this cross-commuting can be eliminated.

At the moment there is no incentive for an employer to look for workers who live close by. Distance from the workplace is no consideration for the employer, providing the workers do a good job and arrive on time. But the whole city would benefit if employers made the distance an employee would travel to work, and by what means, part of their selection criteria. One possible way of encouraging employers to do this would be a simple education program promoting the benefits of employing those who live locally and those who intend to use city-friendly forms of transport. These benefits are obvious. A less congested and a more compact city means a more efficient city for commerce. Competitiveness is improved.

The less obvious benefits are the higher productivity rates of the employees who live closer to work and who are thus less likely to be late or take time off. Local employees have more transportation options in the event of car break-down, transport strikes, etc.

Another way to reduce cross-commuting would be for State, Federal and Local Governments to set up their own internal Job/Home Rationalisation Scheme. Also a Job Exchange Bureau could be established where people could register and be computer-matched for job exchange. The government could even offer a monetary incentive for retraining and would more than recoup this in savings on road maintenance, extra road space, city spread and effects of pollution.

If these voluntary measures were insufficient a Commuter Surcharge/Rebate system could be introduced by placing a surcharge on payroll tax or company income. The rationale for this is that authorities provide the transport infrastructure needed for employers to transport employees to their work place. This is expensive and, at the moment, some employers are abusing the system. The surcharge would be a means of bringing equity into the system and creating a more efficient city so that all businesses can profit.

In order to recoup the Commuter Surcharge, employers would need to actively discourage cross-commuting. This would involve: employing people who lived close to work; convincing their employees to come by public transport, walk or cycle; replacing parking subsidies with an open public transport travel card; persuading employees to move closer to their work place. Alternatively, the employer could provide housing within walking distance of the workplace, or even at the workplace, as part of the salary package.

Each year, companies could be asked to declare how far and by what means employees have come to work. A simple points scoring procedure would then determine how much of the Commuter Surcharge became a Commuter Rebate. It could be constructed so that the scheme was revenue neutral. In other words, those companies who act most responsibly would be refunded more than they had paid, while those who had not acted so responsibly would receive no rebate at all. A great bonus of this scheme would be the detailed information city authorities would gain about commuter traffic. And the results of reducing cross-commuting would be calmer traffic, a more efficient city and a less-strained workforce.

Commuter traffic

Commuter traffic is undoubtedly the biggest single transportation problem in our cities, accounting for about half of all the kilometres travelled by private motorists and one-third of all trips.[18] I suggested that, apart from the gains made possible by reducing cross-commuting, it is possible to cut commuter traffic by half if instead of 1.1 people occupying each car, there were 2.2. Impossible? If there was a national emergency, such as a war, it would happen immediately. But, for now, imagine every suburb had a series of lift-bays, each signposted with a major destination in the city. Cars could not proceed past the lift-bays unless the driver had a letter from the employer or a statutory declaration that the car would be needed during the day for work. Cars leaving the lift-bay area must have at least three people aboard or be cleared by a supervisor. Traffic would drop by almost two-thirds. 'Imagine the chaos at the lift-stations', someone will respond. Would it be any worse than the stop–start peak hour crawls that make journeys three times their normal duration? It is hard to envisage that the delays at the pick-up bays would be any longer than the aggregate delays normally experienced. Once through the pick-up point it would be like travelling normally out of peak times. One could also predict that within a short time people would have made prior arrangements which would mean not going to the pick-up bay. Alternatively, many may decide that public transport offers an easier solution. It would seem that the end result would be that everyone would benefit and no-one would be inconvenienced. More gain with little pain.

Shopping traffic

The local store and local shopping centre play an essential part in the social life of a neighbourhood. Shopping locally is not only important because it cuts down the amount of traffic on the roads, but also because it provides for higher levels of spontaneous exchange which further reduces the need for planned trips and improves the overall quality of life. Not to be overlooked is the effect local shopping has on a just distribution of access to goods and services for non-motorists. The regional shopping centre undermines the viability of the local corner store. The result for those who do not have the ability to access the regional shopping centre is that they have a reduced range of goods, increased prices and often further to walk for them.

Motorists are not paying the true costs of their trip when parking at regional shopping centres. The 'savings' they make on their groceries are paid in increased rates, increased taxes and money taken out of the pockets of the non-motorists.

There are ways to promote neighbourhood shopping. One solution is a simple 'Shop Locally and Save the World' (SLSW) marketing campaign. It could be run by a government body with a steering committee of small business people from across the city, by a non-profit organisation, by local business people or by local residents, or by any combination of these. A number of representatives would visit local businesses inviting them to join in the campaign for a small fee. This would entitle them to place the SLSW sign on the front of their shop and use the logo in their advertising. Each shop would receive a generous supply of brochures entitled, 'How You Can Save the World by Shopping Locally'. The brochure would explain that in most cases shopping at a regional shopping centre is more expensive than shopping locally, once the full running expenses of the car and the hidden costs paid in taxes for urban sprawl are taken into consideration. But it would also stress the many other things that are saved by shopping locally. The sub-headings would tell the story: Shop Locally and Save Money; Shop Locally and Save Time; Shop Locally & Save Your Neighbourhood; Shop Locally

and Save the Environment.

A SLSW coordinator could run workshops and seminars to encourage small businesses in a neighbourhood to join together and explore ways of coaxing people back into shopping locally. Such measures may include running a Neighbourhood Entertainment Night where a small stage is erected and residents invited to provide entertainment. On the fringes small stalls are set up for people to sell such things as produce, outgrown clothes and handicrafts. Money raised from these weekly events would be used to provide permanent seating, landscaping, art, fountains, shade and calming devices for traffic in the local shopping centre.

The authorities could back the SLSW campaign by prohibiting the establishment of any more regional shopping centres on the fringe of the city. Of course, existing regional centres may experience a loss in trade if this campaign was successful. But so be it because the small shop owners and non-car owners have been suffering for decades. The only real beneficiaries have been the regional chain operators, car manufacturers and oil companies. And good uses could be found for the huge car parks and buildings as conference centres, high-tech industrial centres, or urban village developments with a mix of housing, shopping, community centre and employment.

One of the great side benefits of this scheme is employment. High volume turnover in centralised venues employs less people per dollar spent than the same amount spread over a number of stores in local areas. I explained this principle at a public meeting once and a man stood up to tell of his experience in once owning a chain of five shoe stores in local areas employing a total of fifteen people. He closed these down to go into a regional shopping centre where his rent and overheads (such as a commitment to renew the carpet every three years whether it was needed or not) was about the same as for the five stores combined. But he cut his staff needs to five. The total number of shoes sold was about the same but, with slightly lower prices, profit remained about the same. Returning to decentralised marketing would have employed an extra ten people – most of them locally.

Of course, greater local employment will have a snowballing effect. Imagine a neighbourhood in which there is a small specialist delicatessen. Because most people work during the day, the delicatessen receives a flurry of business from 7.00 am to 8.30 am and virtually no trade again till about 4.30 pm when people are coming home from work. Viability of the business is so marginal that the delicatessen owner is thinking of closing. But then a small print shop opens around the corner. Now lunches and snacks are sold to the workers in the part of day when trade was previously dead. The delicatessen owner decides to stay and

advertises the fact by having a flyer printed at the new print shop. A little later someone who makes handcrafted sandals opens a shop down the road. After a few more of these local businesses open, the delicatessen is flourishing. So someone is inspired to open a hot bread kitchen. Each new business that is established not only provides a better range of services for locals, but also provides a ready market for other businesses. Because of the variety of shops, the neighbourhood takes on a character of its own and people from other neighbourhoods come to visit and patronise the specialist stores, increasing the viability of all services even further. Thus diversity attracts diversity and service is added to service.

Such a 'Shop Locally and Save the World' campaign would encourage new services and bring a greater range of goods back into neighbourhoods. Those who rely solely on the local shopping centre gradually gain access to a wider range of goods and services and the quality of life of the entire neighbourhood is improved.

School traffic

School traffic presents one of those vicious cycles which feeds on itself. Parents drive their children to school because it is too dangerous for them to walk. This increases traffic, forcing other parents to drive because it is now too dangerous for *their* children to walk. How can this vicious cycle be broken? One solution may be the Walking Bus.

Parents, police, teachers and authorities map where each child lives in relation to the school and the safest route for these children to go to and from school. Through local papers and other media outlets, volunteers (including senior citizens) are asked to become Walking Bus Drivers. These 'drivers' walk a set route, much like a school bus, collecting children along the route and delivering them safely to school. To increase the profile of the Walking Bus, a coloured line can be painted on the side of the road to indicate where it runs and murals painted on the footpath at the various stops. A trolley can be pulled that would hold raincoats or school ports in the case of rain.

I am sure this scheme would do more than simply see children to school safely and allow parents to stop driving them. If senior citizens were encouraged to take part it would promote a wonderful sense of neighbourhood, especially when so many children today do not have grandparents living close by. It could be the start of a growing sense of place and some invaluable exchanges.

Effecting the change

What public transport authorities have found in the past is that when they try to increase patronage by increasing the quality of service (more frequent services, cheaper fares, better connections, faster service, air conditioning, and more comfortable seating), it takes years for this strategy of service-oriented incentives to have any real effect on convincing people to transfer from private motor vehicles to public transport. The uptake is extremely slow because old habits die hard. When people who normally drive themselves to work wake up in the morning, they do not ask themselves: 'How will I go to work this morning? Should I walk, hitch a ride with a friend or take the bike?' Regardless of how much

the public transport system has been improved, people who are in the habit of driving simply do what they always do: jump in their car. In marketing terms, these people are simply 'not in the market' for a new means of transportation. People only come into the market when their established chain of behaviour is broken into by some external force. This may take the form of the car breaking down, a change of address or even by reading a book such as this that challenges their current behaviour. It is then and only then that they will try a new form of transport. And once they have tried, they may decide that because the bus has leather seats, piped music and is air-conditioned, they will continue with their new arrangement even after the car is fixed. They may even decide to sell the car.

What is needed, then, is some event that breaks the chains of established behaviour. Perhaps a 'Traffic Reduction Day'. This would be similar to 'Leave Your Car at Home Day', 'Public Transport Day' or 'Car Pooling Week', but far more comprehensive and all-invasive. The clear aim is to break existing behaviour patterns and offer positive reinforcement to new modes of behaviour. The lead-up to the day would involve an information campaign to tell people what environmental and social effects traffic has on the city.

Businesses could be targeted, and the economic disadvantages of congested roads and a spreading city spelt out, including the increased cost of transporting goods. They could be asked to do one of a number of things in response: help their employees find alternative ways of going to work on the day; give all workers arriving by other than private motor vehicle (including vehicles carrying four or more people) a half hour early mark on Traffic Reduction Day; or become sponsors of the day. Sponsors could donate prizes or awards such as the person walking the furthest distance to work; the school with the lowest number of cars delivering children; the government department with the lowest number of cars used for commuting in the morning; the person arriving in the city centre on foot in the funniest outfit; or the most unusual form of transport. These could be awarded at a gala event as part of a week of concentrated activities. Other sponsors could provide a free breakfast at city centres for those who arrived by means other than a private motor vehicle.

One incoming lane of all radial routes with four or more lanes could be closed to regular traffic and reserved for walkers, skaters, cyclists and any other form of non-motorised transport. Alternatively, an outgoing lane could be marked off and reserved for this purpose. Free fares could be offered on public transport.

The whole event should be portrayed as a fun event so that traffic reduction has positive connotations and is associated with the positive aspects of city living; culture, social interaction, entertainment, art and celebration. The new patterns of behaviour that emerged on such a day would need positive reinforcement and incentives for people to keep their new forms of behaviour. Fares may be held at half-price for a time. Those walking or riding a bike may go into the draw for a super prize. Prizes may also be given to public transport users.

I can imagine that some people will react unfavourably to the idea of using 'greed' as the motivation for establishing new patterns of behaviour. I once read of a council which tried to persuade residents to sort their rubbish for recycling. The response rate was abysmal. Eventually they offered a weekly $500 cash prize to the first house they came to in a randomly chosen street with rubbish sorted. Suddenly almost everyone started sorting their rubbish. The council commissioned a study in which residents were asked why they sorted their rubbish. Almost without exception the reply was, 'Because it is the environmentally responsible thing to do'; the very line the council had been (unsuccessfully) pushing before the offer of the prize.

What had suddenly made all these people environmentally responsible? Was it pure, unbridled greed? In a minority of cases it may have been. But the majority of people really did want to act responsibly. But this meant breaking their established chain of behaviour which is a difficult thing to do. In marketing terms, they had to 'overcome inertia'. Changing behaviour is like pushing a car. The hardest part is to start it rolling; we often need a little extra help, some extra weight. The thought that they might win $500 was the little extra help these residents needed to overcome their inertia and sort the rubbish.

As well as being given rational reasons why they should change to green modes of transport for commuting, people need some help to overcome the inertia common with all decisions to change an established pattern of behaviour.

Traffic Reduction Day could also be used to launch innovative transportation programs, such as new passes or new services, even measures such as increased parking fees for those arriving in the peak period. This provides a focus for ongoing action. Hopefully, a percentage of those whose chain of behaviour has been broken will make permanent changes. Through a range of promotions and events like this, the Mayor of Erlangen, in Germany, was able to decrease overall traffic by a massive 17 per cent.

With all these proposed radical changes, planners and road engineers may begin to worry about their job security. But these people can be assured that their jobs are safe. The likely scenario is that the government will establish a Department of Traffic Reduction or a Department for Increasing Exchange Efficiency. The goal of this new department will be to reduce traffic and increase exchange by such measures as encouraging greater use of transport other than private motor vehicles, shortening existing journey lengths, car pooling, and more efficient movement of goods. This new department should have its funding tied to performance, this being measured by the drop in average vehicle kilometres per person combined with the drop in public transport deficit per person. It would be given a percentage of the money saved in road maintenance, new road works, urban sprawl, etc. Part of this could be spent on running the department and some on specific programs that will further reduce traffic, for example bikeways, transit lanes or green bridges.

By this funding arrangement, resources devoted to road building and its associated side-effects would be gradually re-allocated to projects that increase exchange efficiency rather than undermining it. Engineers and planners who are currently employed in designing increasing road infrastructure would be transferred to the new department to design and build bike- and walk-ways, green bridges, calming devices around schools and neighbourhood shopping centres. They will be out in the streets interacting with people who are disadvantaged, asking them how to make their neighbourhood an interactive community. They would be part of a growth industry.

Four modest proposals

Seven year moratorium and revitalisation of neighbourhoods
The greatest contribution people can make to building the Eco-City is to foster the health of the city at the micro level. The first proposal is to place a seven year moratorium on the widening of any roads or building of urban freeways in the *existing* built up areas of our cities (roadworks for new residential areas exempted). The money saved could be spent on bringing facilities into neighbourhoods and facilitating exchange-friendly transport infrastructure at the neighbourhood level (promenade loops, pedestrian priority to public transport stops, cycle parking spaces, etc.). Kenneth Schneider gives some idea of the difference this could make:

> In Fresno, the sixty million dollars [1979 figures] that would build only six miles of freeway could construct a million-dollar community centre at every one of the sixty-odd elementary schools in the metropolitan area. Combined with existing school facilities, the new gyms, pools, club rooms, and libraries afforded would provide a magnificent service to every neighbourhood. Yet more than fifty urban miles of freeway were planned in Fresno in the heady freeway years of the early 1960s.[19]

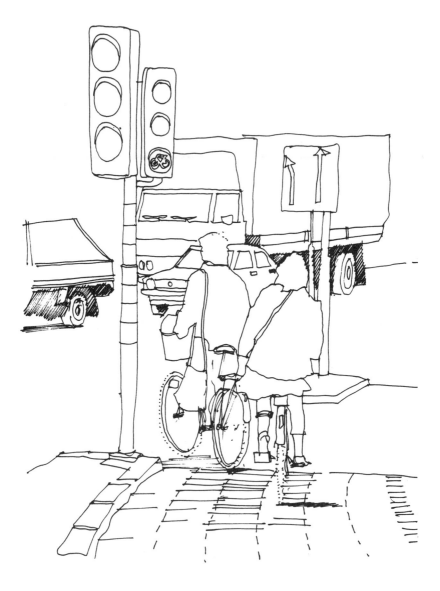

Encouraging exchange-friendly neighbourhood development
The second proposal is to encourage exchange-friendly and neighbour-hood-friendly developments via a variable transit headworks charge on new developments and a variable transit rates on all land. In a draft paper on the future of Los Angeles transit, Joel Woodhull argued that developers should pay for the transport infrastructure needed to cater for the trips they generate and that this should be used to provide public transport for the trips generated. 'Something of the order of $5,000 per daily trip generated by the development would provide the transit subsidy required to service that trip in perpetuity'.[20]

Rather than a blanket transit headworks charge, I would suggest a variable charge that decreases according to how exchange-friendly the development is. The developer could earn credits for the following:

- *Pedestrian friendliness:* provision of pedestrian facilities outside the building such as seating, shade, fountains, sculptures, activity centres like outdoor chess boards; wheelchair and pram access; provision of mid-block pedestrian walkways;

- *Cycle friendliness:* safe storage, showers, priority access;

- *Neighbourhood friendliness:* reductions for mixed use (residential and business in one building); greater reductions for those servicing local neighbourhoods than those servicing regional needs (on the basis that people must travel *further* for regional facilities which requires greater infrastructure); discounts according to the degree to which the development fills identified gaps in local facilities.

This last point needs some explanation. The relevant government department would work with local communities to identify their most pressing needs for making their neighbourhoods more self-sufficient, for example, a cinema, hairdresser, butcher shop or community activity centre. If a developer includes one or more of these identified needs then they earn credits against their transit headworks charge.

In a similar way, a section of what is now general land rates on all properties becomes a *variable transit rate*, calculated to be the percentage of rates which goes to providing and maintaining transport infrastructure. Properties (including residential) would be scored for their exchange friendliness in a similar way as were the headworks charges. On residential properties, such things as size of block and number of cars owned by residents would be taken into account. Commercial property developers who modified buildings to make them more pedestrian, cycle or neighbourhood friendly would earn a permanent discount in the transit rate.

City-wide calming

My third proposal is for city-wide calming. The current Local Area Traffic Management (LATM) schemes can never hope to provide a traffic-calmed street environment for the majority of city dwellers. Three things stand in the way. Firstly, the massive cost of treating the whole city with LATM measures. Secondly, impetuous drivers who see such environments as challenges to their driving skill; for example, how fast can they go over the speed bumps or zigzag through the landscape. Thirdly, the social justice issues of pushing even more traffic onto already busy residential streets which have been labeled as 'collector', 'sub-arterial' or 'arterial'. What is clearly needed is a measure which does not rely solely on changing the physical structure of the street and one which can be introduced city wide. LATMs should continue as a means of improving the beauty of the street environment but they cannot be seen as the solution for calming traffic.

This third proposal is built on the observation that it is the *driver*, not the street, who needs calming and that there is a small percentage of the motoring population, the aggressive drivers, causing the majority of noise and safety problems. Through introduction of mobile speed cameras throughout the city (Stage One), the majority of these problem drivers would be caught in the first one or two years of this scheme. Instead of fining these drivers, they would be required to fit a manually set speed limiter (a device which limits the top speed of the vehicle and can be varied by the driver with the flick of a switch). A digital read out, showing at what speed the limiter is set, must be displayed in the back window of the car or near the number plate. If they are caught by a speed camera a second time and the display is set at the wrong speed, then severe penalties similar to those applying to drunk-driving would be imposed. Stage Two of the scheme would encourage all people to fit speed limiters by offering registration discounts. Stage Three would be to install transponders (an electronic device) on the side of the road wherever the speed limit changes. The transponder sends out a signal which would automatically set the speed limiter in the car to the appropriate speed.

The obvious advantages of this scheme would be the increased safety. Based on overseas experience with large areas of traffic-calmed streets, one could expect a 50–80 per cent fall in deaths and injuries, together with a drop in noise and pollution levels. The less obvious advantage is that it would increase the attractiveness of public transport. Car speeds could be dropped down as low as 20 kilometres per hour in special zones such as around schools and shopping centres, 30 kilometres per hour on residential streets and 50 kilometres per hour on major arterials. Meanwhile, buses could travel in transit lanes at much higher speeds, thus removing one of the perceived advantages of the private car – faster

travelling times and the ability to speed in order to arrive sooner.

Experimental car-free urban villages
The fourth proposal is to set up experimental car-free urban villages. Clearly, most people must experience an alternative before they can imagine its potential. Governments should work with private developers to construct an urban village which not only has all the features advocated so far in this book, but is also car free. Internal transport would be by electric mini-buses, electric delivery carts, walking and cycling. Transport to the outside world would be by fast, efficient public transport or community owned electric hire cars. Advantages to the developer would be far greater yield for the amount of land. Advantages to residents would be a wider range of services, no traffic noise, clean air and a totally safe environment. It is my perception that there would be a huge market for such a development including those who cannot drive, do not want to drive, or would be prepared to give it up if they saw a positive alternative.

The car-free urban village would be an educational tool. When people came to visit friends, they would experience first-hand the incredible advantages of such an environment. While they may not demand to be able to live in a similar place, they may well make demands about how car usage could be reduced in their own neighbourhoods.

All of the above proposals are modest and achievable. In a space of five to 15 years the whole urban landscape could be transformed.

Feeding the Eco-City revolution

You may be a victim of the auto-city already. Footpaths are narrowed and gardens and front rooms have become uninhabitable places due to the spreading zone-of-influence. Walking and cycling spaces may be hostile and unsafe and neighbourhood stores may have long gone. Places have become spaces and you are forced to travel further than you need to. Someone from across town probably has the job near your home and you are forced to act as chauffeur to your children. The spontaneous exchanges you may once have enjoyed with neighbours in the street may have mysteriously disappeared and the colour, the diversity and the spontaneity may have been drained from your neighbourhood.

Perhaps your neighbourhood is currently under threat. Your city council may be planning a freeway through your area or the widening of a road through your shopping centre. Or you may have a vision of what your city could be like and simply want to help build the Eco-City.

I do not propose to discuss the tactics for waging a community battle here; that would take another book. But the lessons learnt from CART's battle, particularly those learnt from the mistakes we have made, may prove invaluable for other groups.

Personal action

What can you do as an individual? Before anything else, the three most important things you can do are:

1. Go for a walk around your neighbourhood.

2. Go for a walk around your neighbourhood.

3. Go for a walk around your neighbourhood.

While you walk, there are four important things to do which will be the seeds of the revolution: say hello to the people you meet; with each step you take say, 'This is my neighbourhood'; dream of what your neighbourhood could be like based on what you have learnt from this book; decide in what ways you will help make your neighbourhood an interactive community.

In fulfilling this last step you may find yourself contemplating the way our society has made a god of the automobile and is obsessed with the saving of time. Whatever your thoughts, there are a number of reasons why I have suggested three walks around your neighbourhood. The first is that Western society has a pre-occupation with bringing about reform through structural changes (making the city a better machine). They perceive an injustice and immediately want to organise a committee to fight it and change the system. Unfortunately, there is often a failure to analyse the true causes of the problem which are more often than not deeply rooted in people's lives, culture, and values. Structural changes are important, but as Robert Pirsig put it: 'The place to improve the world is first in one's heart and hands, and then outward from there'.[21]

This struck home to me, in the middle of the Route 20 battle, when I realised that my use of the car had increased dramatically as I raced around having brochures printed, making arrangements, and going to meetings. I was fighting a freeway by using a car more. I did the only thing I could – bought a bike so I could carry on the work but without the dramatic increase in car usage.

Real changes to the city will only happen through a process of people calming which will spring from a change in the way we view ourselves and our city. Those changes of values and ethos must take root somewhere, and where better than in the people arguing for them.

Group action

Most community action groups never accomplish their goals because they do not know where they are going or how to get there. I was once asked by a group to talk to them about strategies they might use to fight a freeway proposed for their suburb. I asked them if they had in their minds a course of events which might lead to them winning. They replied that they had never really thought about it because they did not think they had any chance of winning. By their own admission their fight was a token one and they were beaten before they started. My advice to them was to work through the following process:

■ Define the objective by asking, what is to be accomplished?

■ Analyse the current situation and determine what the real problems are. Learn everything there is to know about your 'opponents'. For instance, what motivates them, what is their personal position, and what are the power plays amongst them. Understand the position of those you are fighting with and for. Are they demoralised and unwilling to fight? If so, why?

■ Brainstorm all possible scenarios for reaching your objective by asking the question: What possible chain of events could result in our reaching our objective? The raw data collected from the previous step becomes the basis for the answer to this question. All scenarios must lie in the realm of possibilities.

■ Settle on a plan by choosing the most promising scenario. It is important to talk about all possible outcomes of each stage of the plan and to draw up contingency plans for each possible outcome.

153

- Break the plan up into manageable pieces and start implementing them.

What happens in real life is that the plan has to be adapted and changed once you start. Some strategists, therefore, think that this kind of process is a waste of time. But the real value of this process is not in the wonderful theoretical plan that evolves, but in the hope it generates, the understanding of the 'opposition', and in the taking of one purposeful step. Suddenly, participants can see one or more ways through the fog. The tune changes from, 'We can't win but we'll give them a hell of a fight', to, 'Hey, we can win'.

Empower people
I explained earlier how whole communities can be gripped with a paralysing sense of hopelessness and futility and that the primary job of a community action group is to empower these people by engendering hope and strengthening their will to take control. Every move our group made in the early stages of our campaign was made with one eye on the 'enemy' and one on the community we were fighting for. One of the first things we did was to screen print a sign on stiff plastic that simply read 'Route 20 Freeway – No Thanks'. We asked residents to buy one and nail it to their front fence. Our motivation was twofold. Firstly, in picking up the hammer to nail the sign on the fence they were breaking the chains of powerlessness. They were taking control and doing something about their plight. At the same time the nailing of their sign was an empowering process to the rest of the community. As 2,000 signs

went up like mushrooms, people were constantly reminded that there were others out there just as angry as they were and that these people were also taking a stand. They were not alone in their anger, or their hope.

Secondly, the signs sent a message to the politicians. As one politician remarked: 'You don't need an opinion poll to tell what the people along Route 20 feel about the proposal. Just drive through the area'. The same effect can be achieved with bumper stickers or even the simple act of tying coloured ribbons on trees, fences, poles, etc.

Empowerment is part of the reason I started this section by suggesting the three walks around your neighbourhood. It is important to give people something easy and symbolic yet meaningful to do if you are to build a mass movement. It is the tactic Gandhi used when he told the people to spin their own cloth. Another important part of this empowering process is to give people the opportunity to share their insights and provide a stimulating context in which people can think through the issues and brainstorm creative solutions. This may take the form of community planning days, debates or the use of community arts.

Create your own media

Recently I attended a workshop for community action groups at which a television current affairs producer outlined the criterion he used to choose the news items. The whole workshop group was upset when the producer admitted that the primary consideration was entertainment value. He admitted that the reason so much bad news is covered is because people like to come home after a rugged day in the work-place, lock their security grill and, from the safe vantage point of their home, watch all the bad things that are happening outside. The people present damned the producer, saying it confirmed all their worst fears about the media. These people were romantics – not realists. They saw the media as the knight in white armour who had turned traitor. But the role of the mass media has always been to capture, via entertainment, audiences for businesses to ply their wares. To believe otherwise is fantasy.

From the beginning of our campaign we only ever saw two roles for the mass media: to empower residents and to send a message to politicians. Rarely did we attempt to use it to educate. This is because you have no control over how the subject matter is presented. More often than not, the media leave out the essential facts and twist the story. But if your goal is simply to empower residents and put pressure on politicians then the content of the story is almost irrelevant, the important thing is the effect of being there. There is truth in the old adage that 'any publicity is good publicity' – as long as it is truthful.

Empowering of residents takes place because of the value the residents put on the six o'clock news. Group members say, 'Did you see we were in the news again. Isn't it great? We are really starting to get places now'. Politicians also believe in the myth of the media, so they believe that those groups who make it onto the six o'clock news must have 'power'.

So if the mass media is not a good medium for education, how does a community group go about educating residents and the general public? By creating their own media. The importance of this can be best explained by the experiences gained from our first newspaper. Part of our plan was to have the whole community involved in the fight against Route 20, not just the few hundred who lived along the actual corridor, many of whom were elderly, short-term renters or people who were totally dispirited. So we decided to publish a newspaper, the aim being to motivate the whole community into becoming involved.

The paper contained a major article on the cancer of urban blight explaining how all the district eventually would be affected. In contrast to this, we built up a sense of pride in the community by having quotes of what people said they liked about the area and a major historical feature that traced the area from its first suburban settlement. The results of this paper were amazing. Within weeks the committee ranks had been swelled by respondents, most of whom were not even affected by the proposal. Some even lived two or three kilometres away.

A side note to this story shows the importance we placed on using the media to empower people and startle the politicians. We had an official launch of the newspaper by carrying the 30,000 copies to a park in the centre of the local shopping centre and building a small mountain out of the papers. We then got two elderly people who would lose part of their yards to cut a ribbon tied around the large pile of papers. The message we were trying to convey through this media event was not, 'please get involved because the cancer of urban blight is coming your way'. That message needed eight tabloid pages to be conveyed properly. No, the message was simply: 'Look at this mountain of newspapers we as a community have produced. We are taking back control'. Other newspapers and the book Traffic Calming were all produced at significant points of our campaign – always when we had a significant message to convey.

Have a positive alternative

In *The Death and Life of Great American Cities*, Jane Jacobs gives some invaluable advice about working towards the attrition of automobiles in cities. She explains that city eroders always couch their proposals in positive terms; they never talk of eroding mobility choices of the elderly, or taking children's play space or narrowing footpaths. They talk about

increasing efficiency, speed and convenience.[22]

Thus in this book I have presented a positive vision. As well as showing the price we pay for our belief in the myth of motion and our enslavement to a mechanistic and materialist culture which has degraded our cities and dehumanised their citizens, I have shown that there is a much more positive alternative in eco-relational thinking and the Eco-City.

Move from confrontation to partnership
Western culture is deeply adversarial. Our judicial system, our parliamentary system, our sport, our commerce, our community life, are all built on the notion of competition and opposition where one party stands against another. We need an 'enemy'.

But in the Eco-City which we are striving to build, the underlying assumption is mutuality and partnership. The battle in the Eco-City is not against fellow inhabitants, but against the ideas and values that would drag us back to the swamp. Only for the first couple of months of our Route 20 battle did I see planners and engineers as the 'enemy'. I quickly came to see that the real opponent was within me. Sure the enemy was also within many of the individuals who made up the planning and engineering profession. But it was first and foremost within me and my fellow residents. Recognising this truth helped us move from initial confrontation to a growing sense of partnership.

If humanity is not to destroy planet Earth, then it is obvious that we need new thought forms to take us into the new millennium. It is time for all people, 'professional' or 'lay', to put aside their differences and work together in battling the real enemy: outdated thinking patterns and outdated attitudes to ourselves and our cities.

Will it be a long road home?

When Edward Lorenz gave birth to the science of chaos with his toy weather world, he discovered, via a one-part-in-a-thousand mistake, that very small changes could blow up into major consequences: the butterfly effect. Lorenz's story not only explains the technical nature of social change, but also illustrates, practically, the nature of change. Newtonian thinking has affected the way we perceive social change which is seen as a linear process, incremental and slow. But even a casual glance at the history books shows that social change does not happen in this fashion. It happens in revolutions.

Social change is like watching an old-fashioned grocer weighing out candy. A weight is placed on one side of the scales (resistance to change) and the candies are dropped one at a time into the container on the other side (reasons to change). As each piece of candy is added nothing happens. But then the grocer adds one more piece of candy and suddenly the balance changes. A 'critical mass' is reached and the balance changes without warning.

The scales may illustrate one aspect of social change – the sudden revolution – but they do not illustrate the speed with which these revolutions occur because the candies are put on the scales one at a time. In social change, as in nature, there is a process of bifurcation. One person has a new idea and tells another, those two tell two and two becomes four, becomes eight, becomes sixteen, becomes thirty-two, and so on.

Whether bifurcation takes place depends very much on the surrounding conditions. The flap of a butterfly's wings do not always produce a hurricane; social revolutions happen when the climate is right. One person thinking a creative thought and planting it at the right time can set off a chain of events that in a very short time changes the whole of history. Newton and Descartes both did it; so have other great philosophers of the past. And even attitudes to passive smoking changed quickly when it was connected to the rights of non-smokers.

One action can also change history. Lorenz, for instance, types some numbers into a computer and gives birth to a science that overthrows the assumptions of Newton and Descartes. Human agents of social change are those who can intuitively read the 'signs of the times'. They learn how to foster the climate in which bifurcation begins to take place.

The seeds of the ecological revolution are being planted everywhere and it matters little where or how they have been planted. All around the world those seeds are in the process of sprouting and giving birth to new life forms. One of those new life forms will be the Eco-City. As I talk with planners and engineers around Australia I realise that this revolution in thinking has already begun. Many recognise the limitations of the past and are grappling with better ways for the future.

The tide has turned. According to Charles Birch, what we are witnessing is a 'radical transformation of science, religion and culture that constitutes a revolution even greater than the Scientific Revolution and the Enlightenment'.[23] The most important frontier in this ecological revolution will be our cities, for the city is the ultimate expression of our science, our religion and our culture. In the soupy smog that hangs over our cities, ideas are colliding, new relationships forming, new life emerging. The volcanoes of vested self-interest may try to annihilate the emerging life form, just as they did a billion years ago, but life will once again triumph and from the chaos will emerge a new life form, the Eco-City.

Appendix A
A draft charter of access-to-exchange rights

The Charter of Access-to-Exchange Rights which follows is a first draft which needs to be subjected to detailed community debate.

Charter of Access-To-Exchange Rights

This bill recognises the inherent dignity and equal worth of all humans regardless of race, age, social status, income, physical ability, religion or any other factor that makes one person or group of people different from others.

It also recognises that while all humans are born with equal worth, not all are born with equal opportunity. This inequality of opportunity places some people or groups of people in a position of strength relative to others. This strength is sometimes used to exploit and oppress rather than to enrich.

This bill therefore recognises that society at all levels has a duty to protect the powerless, ensure a just distribution of all commodities produced or available to a society and encourage the building of interactive communities which encourage each person to use their strengths to enrich others rather than exploiting them.

This bill applies and amplifies rights already recognised in the Universal Declaration of Human Rights, namely:

Article 22
Everyone, as a member of society, has the right to social security and is entitled to realisation, through national effort and international cooperation and in accordance with the organisation and resources of each State, of the economic, social and cultural rights indispensable for his dignity and the free development of his personality.

Article 24
Everyone has the right to rest and leisure...

161

Article 27

Everyone has the right freely to participate in the cultural life of the community, to enjoy the arts and to share in scientific advancement and its benefits.

Article 29

Everyone has duties to the community in which alone the free and full development of his personality is possible.

This Declaration of Access-to-Exchange Rights recognises that transportation is a means by which people gain access to exchange opportunities: 'cultural life', 'the arts' and 'scientific advancements' (article 27); the 'resources of each State' for the realisation of 'economic, social and cultural rights' (article 22); facilities for 'rest and leisure' (article 24); and the means by which people can discharge their 'duties' to the community (article 29).

It further recognises that unless there is equality of opportunity for access to transportation, it is impossible for society to fulfil its obligations as spelt out in the articles cited above.

This bill also recognises that modern day traffic can severely limit people's right to 'rest and leisure' in their own neighbourhood (article 24); can severely limit the possibility of some people freely participating 'in the cultural life of the community' (article 27); and can severely limit the ability of some people to discharge their 'duties to the community' (article 29).

Access-to-Exchange Rights:

Article 1

All people have a right to a just and equitable share in the exchange opportunities which a city can reasonably provide and no person or group in society has the right to improve their share of these exchange opportunities at the expense of another person or group unless this action is necessary to right an existing unjust distribution.

(i) Pedestrians and cyclists have a right to preferential treatment over motorised traffic for funding, access rights and space and where private motorists are granted the privilege of sharing street space with pedestrians and cyclists, the pedestrian and cyclist has right of way over private motor vehicles at all times.

(ii) Pedestrians and cyclists have a right of access to all community and public facilities whether privately or publicly owned and shall not be cut off, hindered or disadvantaged in reaching these destinations by vehicular traffic.

(iii) Pedestrians and cyclists have a right to safe passage at all times.

(iv) No pedestrian or cyclist should be unduly disadvantaged because of handicap, age or because they must push a child in a pram.

(v) Public transport users have a right not to be unduly hindered, delayed or have their service downgraded by private motorists.

(vi) Public transport users have a right to equality of service regardless of race, creed, financial status, age or physical disability and society has a duty to make special provisions for those whose mobility choices are limited by physical condition so that their accessibility is not unduly restricted.

Article 2

No person should be forced because of station in life (social, physical, financial, age, locality, race) to bear an unequal share of the social, environmental or monetary costs of other people's travel.

Article 3

All people have a right to an urban environment that best encourages social, spiritual, intellectual, cultural, emotional and physical well-being and helps an individual develop to their fullest potential.

(i) All people have a right to have their interaction with family, friends and acquaintances protected from restrictions imposed by traffic.

(ii) All people have a right to have their social interaction, recreational activities and sleep protected from excessive noise intrusion.

(iii) All people have a right to the full use of their home and yard and shall not have this space subjugated by noise intrusion.

(iv) All people have a right to clean air free from man-made pollutants which may pose health problems.

(v) Every child has a right to independent safe passage to school, play space for interaction with friends and other facilities essential for their development. Every child also has the right to explore their neighbourhood in ever increasing circles, in safety, as they mature and not be impeded in developing a relationship with their neighbourhood and physical environment.

(vi) Every child has a right to not have their education impeded by excessive noise.

Article 4

All people have first priority use of the living space (street) in front of their homes with rights for others to use that space decreasing in proportion to the distance they live from the street space. Responsibility to act as a guest while using a street increases in proportion to the distance a person lives from the space.

Article 5
All vulnerable people have a right to extra vigilance from the community to protect all of the above rights on their behalf.

The European charter of pedestrians' rights

Adopted by the
European Parliament in 1988

I. The pedestrian has the right to live in a healthy environment and freely to enjoy the amenities offered by public areas under conditions that adequately safeguard his physical and psychological well-being.

II. The pedestrian has the right to live in urban or village centres tailored to the needs of the motor car and to have amenities within walking or cycling distance.

III. Children, the elderly and the disabled have the right to expect towns to be places of easy social contact and not places that aggravate their inherent weakness.

IV. The disabled have the right to specify measures to maximise their independent mobility, including adjustments in public areas, transport systems and public transport (guidelines, warning signs, acoustic signals, accessible buses, trams and trains).

V. The pedestrian has the right to urban areas which are intended exclusively for his use, are as extensive as possible and are not mere 'pedestrian precincts' but in harmony with the overall organisation of the town, and also the exclusive right to connecting short, logical and safe routes.

VI. The pedestrian has a particular right to expect:

(a) compliance with chemical and noise emission standards for motor vehicles which scientists consider to be tolerable;

(b) the introduction into all public transport systems of vehicles that are not a source of either air or noise pollution;

(c) the creation of 'green lungs', including the planting of trees in urban areas;

(d) the fixing of speed limits and modification to the layout of roads and junctions as a way of effectively safeguarding pedestrians and bicycle traffic;

(e) the banning of advertising which encourages an improper and dangerous use of the motor car;

(f) an effective system of road signs whose design also takes into account the needs of children;

(g) the adoption of specific measures to ensure that vehicular pedestrian traffic has ease of access to, and freedom of movement and the possibility of stopping on, roads and pavements respectively;

(h) adjustments to the shape and equipment of motor vehicles so as to give a smoother line to those parts which project most and to make signalling systems more efficient;

(i) the introduction of the system of risk liability so that the person creating the risk bears the financial consequences thereof;

(j) a drivers' training program designed to encourage suitable conduct on the roads in respect of pedestrians and other slow road users.

VII. The pedestrian has the right to complete and unimpeded mobility, which can be achieved through the integrated use of the means of transport. In particular, he has the right to expect:

(a) an ecologically sound, extensive and well-equipped public transport service which will meet the needs of all citizens, from the physically fit to the disabled;

(b) the provision of facilities for bicycles throughout the urban areas;

(c) parking lots which are sited in such a way that they affect neither the mobility of pedestrians nor their ability to enjoy areas of architectural distinction.

VIII. Each Member State must ensure that comprehensive information of the rights of pedestrians and on alternative ecologically sound forms of transport is disseminated through the most appropriate channels and is made available to children from the beginning of their school career.

Glossary

Accessibility: The ease with which exchange opportunities can be accessed.

City: A concentration of diverse people, goods and facilities within a limited area and brought together in order to widen the choice of exchange opportunities while decreasing the need for travel.

Cross-commuting: Person A and Person B, who both have the same type of job, each commuting to work in the other person's suburb.

Eco-City: A people-made eco-system (city) created to enable all participants to reach their fullest potential by maximising exchanges and minimising travel.

Eco-relational view: Belief that phenomena can only be understood by discerning the complex, interdependent web of relationships in an eco-system. An holistic or systemic view. The opposite of mechanistic, reductionist thinking.

Eco-system: A community of organisms and their environment interacting and interdependent as in a rainforest.

Exchange: The mutual giving and receiving which enriches all elements within an eco-system.

Exchange efficiency: The efficiency with which exchanges are achieved – total costs (time and resources) divided by total exchanges.

Exchange opportunities: Potential exchanges which residents of the Eco-City can avail themselves of.

Exchange space: Places which facilitate exchanges. See Placeness and Movement space.

Fractal: An arrangement of parts so that, no matter at what scale the object is viewed, it appears the same.

Generalist: Someone who thinks holistically across the artificial boundaries of specialisation, having a general knowledge spanning many subjects.

Holistic thinking: See Eco-relational view.

Home-based access: Accessing exchange opportunities in the home environment without the recipient needing to travel; for example, home deliveries, the telephone and tele-commuting. See Planned access and Spontaneous access.

Home-based exchange: The exchanges that take place in the home environment without the recipient needing to travel. See Planned exchange and Spontaneous exchange.

Home territory: The area around a person's home which is considered to be an extension of the home and over which there is some sense of ownership and psychological connection.

Mechanistic thinking: Viewing everything in the universe as a machine governed by pre-determined laws. Closely connected to reductionist thinking (reducing everything to their base building blocks) and materialism (the belief that the only real thing is matter). See Eco-relational view.

Mono-culture: A system devoid of diversity. The opposite of the rich diversity found in an eco-system.

Mono-cultural cities: Cities which have eliminated diversity or 'fenced off' different cultures into 'mono-cultural fields'.

Movement space: Space in a city dedicated to facilitating movement of people and goods in order to facilitate exchanges. See Exchange space.

Placeness: Those ingredients which transform a space into a place by facilitating and enhancing exchanges between the elements of that place and those elements which enter it.

Planned access: Deliberately taking a trip for the purpose of gaining access to an exchange opportunity. For example, making an appointment to see the doctor and getting in the car to drive there. See Spontaneous access and Home-based access.

Planned exchange: Exchange transacted at the end of a planned journey. See Spontaneous exchange and Home-based exchange.

Postmodern world view: A world view which rejects the mechanistic and reductionist thinking ushered in by the Industrial and Scientific Revolutions and embraces an holistic, systemic view.
See Eco-relational view.

Reductionist thinking: Belief that a complex phenomenon or event can be explained by analysing and describing its individual parts. See Mechanistic thinking and Eco-relational thinking.

Setting deprivation: There are archetypal places that facilitate certain types of exchange (for example, sense of identity) which are essential for the well-being of a person. When a person is completely denied access to a particular type of space, they are denied a particular kind of exchange and hence suffer setting deprivation.

Spontaneous access: Accidentally encountering an exchange opportunity – usually when making a trip for some other purpose; for example, bumping into a friend when walking to the corner store. See Planned access and Home-based access.

Spontaneous exchange: Exchanges that take place when an exchange opportunity is encountered accidentally; for example, the information and psychological support exchanged when two friends accidentally meet when walking to the corner store. See Planned exchange and Home-based exchange.

Spreading-city syndrome: City spread triggered by conversion of exchange space into movement space which automatically requires more travel to maintain preivous levels of exchange – which then requires a further transformation of exchange space to movement space.

Sustainability: The ability of future generations to be able to reach their full potential in all areas of their humanity by having access to sufficient and diverse natural, social and cultural resources, passed on by the current generation.

Tele-commuting: Working from home and being connected to the normal workplace via telecommunications links such as telephone, fax, and computer.

Traffic calming: Management of the movement of people and goods in order to maximise exchanges while minimising travel along with the social and environmental effects of travel.

Urban blight: A cancerous process which destroys or saps the vibrancy of a neighbourhood. The catalyst for the process can be the dividing of a neighbourhood by a freeway, excessive traffic or an inappropriate development.

Zone-of-influence: The area over which traffic extends its influence via noise, fumes, vibration, threat to safety and destruction of the elements of placeness.

Endnotes

Introduction

1 David Engwicht (ed.), *Traffic Calming – The Solution to Route 20 and a New Vision for Brisbane*, CART, Brisbane, 1989.

2 David Engwicht, 'Access Efficiency Enhancement – More Saleable Than "Demand Management" & Providing a New Suite of System-wide Indicators', *1991 International Transport Conference – Preprints of Papers*, Institute of Engineers, Australia National Conference Publication no. 91/4, Canberra, 1991, pp. 1–8

1   The nature of the Eco-City

1 Cited, Peter Hall, *Cities of Tomorrow*, Basil Blackwell, Oxford, 1988, p. 47

2 Kenneth R. Schneider, *On the Nature of Cities*, Jossey-Bass Publication, San Francisco, 1979, p. 25

3 Bernard Rudofsky, *Streets for People – A Primer for Americans*, Doubleday & Company, New York, 1969, pp. 123–132

4 Conducted at the 1991 International Transport Conference. The question was: 'Complete this sentence. The role of transport in the city is...'. Responses were:

Movement of people and goods	29%*
Access	24%
Facilitate high standard of living	14%**
Facilitate commercial activities	12%*
Facilitate interaction or exchange	11%
Delivery to work	8%**

   * Responses where 'free movement' is the key concept
   ** Responses where 'free movement' is an underlying concept
Responses may have been biased through some delegates having received my paper the night before which argued that the goal of transport was exchange not movement.

5 Jane Jacobs, *The Death and Life of Great American Cities*, Random House, New York, 1961.

6 Lewis Mumford wrote extensively and many of his quotes in this book are drawn from secondary sources. I found *The Myth of the Machine*, Harcourt, Brace & World, New York, 1967, very stimulating.

7 Charles Birch, *On Purpose*, New South Wales University Press, Sydney, 1990, p. 83

8 Roberto Brambilla, *More Streets for People*, The Italian Art and Landscape Foundation, 1975, p. 14

171

9   Cited, Geoff Lacey, *What Technologies Are Appropriate?*, Pax Christi, Carlton South, Melbourne, 1989, pp. 4–5

10 ibid.

11 Peter Hall, *Cities of Tomorrow*, Basil Blackwell, Oxford, 1988, p. 48

12 Peter Newman & Jeffrey Kenworthy, *Cities and Automobile Dependence – An International Source Book*, Gower Technical, Aldershot, 1989, p. 93

13 Schneider, op.cit., p. 74

14 Reinhold Mähler, 'Pedestrian Malls: Symbols of Citizen-Oriented Planning', *Proceedings: Fifth Annual Pedestrian Conference*, Transportation Division, City of Boulder, Boulder, 1984, p. 57

15 Jan Tanghe, Sieg Vlaeminck & Jo Berghoef, *Living Cities*, Pergamon Press, Oxford, 1984, p. 71

16 John Roberts, 'Genius Loci – How Is It Retained or Revived?', *Proceedings: Eighth Annual Pedestrian Conference*, City of Boulder Transport Division, Boulder, 1987, p. 90

17 For the ideas behind five of these ingredients I am indebted to a paper by Henry L. Lennard & Suzanne Crowhurst Lennard, 'Ethics of Public Space', *Stepping Out in Urban Design – Proceedings: Sixth Annual Pedestrian Conference*, Transportation Division, City of Boulder, Boulder, 1985, pp. 137–141

18 ibid., p. 138

19 Schneider, op.cit., p. 138

20 Lewis Mumford, *The Myth of the Machine*, Harcourt, Brace & World, New York, 1967, pp. 7–8

21 ibid., p. 54

22 From 'Aanzet todt een stedebouwkundige theorie' quoted in Tanghe et al, op.cit., p. 140

23 Henry L. Lennard & Suzanne Crowhurst Lennard, 'Ethics of Public Space', *Stepping Out in Urban Design – Proceedings: Sixth Annual Pedestrian Conference*, Transportation Division, City of Boulder, Boulder, 1985, p. 138

24 ibid., p. 137

25 Dan Burden, 'Getting There', *Proceedings: Seventh Annual Pedestrian Conference*, Transport Division, City of Boulder, Boulder, 1986. 39

26 Kenneth R Schneider, *On the Nature of Cities*, Jossey-Bass Publication, San Francisco, 1979. 307-308

27 Tanghe et al, op.cit., p. 166

28 Cited, Schneider, op.cit., p. 204

2   How traffic destroys the Eco-City

1   Cited, TEST, *Quality Streets*, TEST, London, 1988.

2   Cited, David St. Clair, *The Motorization of American Cities*, Praeger, New York, 1986, p. 166

3   Peter Newman, 'An Ecological Model for City Structure and Development', *Ekistics* 239, October 1975, Athens Technological Organization, Athens Centre of Ekistics, Athens, 1975, p. 258

4 Cited, Steve Clark, 'Putting Pedestrians on a Pedestal: Ways to Rise Above the Tide of Vehicular Chauvinism', *Proceedings: Eighth Annual Pedestrian Conference*, City of Boulder Transportation Division, Boulder, 1987, p. 165

5 Michael Renner, *Rethinking the Role of the Automobile*, Worldwatch Paper 84, Worldwatch Institute, Washington D.C., 1988, p. 46

6 Ian Manning, *Beyond Walking Distance – The Gains from Speed in Australian Urban Travel*, Urban Research Unit, Australian National University, Canberra, 1984, p. 42

7 ibid., p. 22

8 Patrick Moriarty & Clive Beed, 'Reducing Vehicular Travel Need Through Increasing Travel Efficiency', *Urban Policy and Research*, vol. 7, no. 4, Oxford University Press, South Melbourne, 1989, p. 161

9 Manning, op.cit., p. 86

10 Donald Appleyard, *Livable Streets*, University of California Press, Berkeley, 1981.

11 ibid., p. 22

12 ibid., p. 22–24

13 ibid., p. 26

14 P. Lacoute, *The Environment of Human Settlement: Human Well-being in Cities*, Pergamon, Oxford, 1976, p. 182

15 Appleyard, op.cit., p. 27

16 ibid.

17 Jane Jacobs, *The Death and Life of Great American Cities*, Random House, New York, 1961, p. 46

18 Cited, Jan Tanghe, Sieg Vlaeminck & Jo Berghoef, *Living Cities*, Pergamon Press, Oxford, 1984, p. 76

19 James Gleick, *Chaos – Making a New Science*, Sphere Books, London, 1990, pp. 11–31

20 ibid., p. 15

21 ibid., p. 12

22 T. Cartwright, 'Planning and Chaos Theory', *Journal of the American Planning Association*, vol. 57, no. 1, Winter 1991, American Planning Association, Chicago, 1991, p. 53

23 Graham Perry, 'Family Suburb Destroyed', *Route 20 News no. 1*, CART, Brisbane, 1987, p. 3

24 Marshall Berman, 'Among the Ruins', *New Internationalist*, Dec 1987, New Internationalist Publications, Melbourne, 1987, pp. 8–9

3 Eco-relational thinking

1 Laurence Stephan Cutler & Sherrie Stephens-Cutler, 'Establishing a Dialog for Recycling Cities', *Ekistics*, 256 March 1977, Athens Technological Organisation, Athens Centre of Ekistics, Athens, 1977, p. 167

2 Zechariah 8:3–5, *Good News Bible*, 1976

3 Matthew Fox, *Original Blessing*, Bear and Company, Santa Fe, New Mexico, 1986, p. 176

4 Jane Jacobs, *The Death and Life of Great American Cities*, Random House, New York, 1961, p. 407

5 Saul D Alinsky, *Rules for Radicals*, Random House, New York, 1971, p. 105

6 James Gleick, *Chaos – Making a New Science*, Sphere Books, London, 1990, p. 230

7 Jan Tanghe, Sieg Vlaeminck & Jo Berghoef *Living Cities*, Pergamon Press, Oxford, 1984, pp. 93–94

8 Lewis Mumford, *The Myth of the Machine*, Harcourt, Brace & World, New York, 1967, p. 87

4   Eco-rights

1 Kenneth R. Schneider, *On the Nature of Cities*, Jossey-Bass Publication, San Francisco, 1979, p. 303

2 Cited, John Roberts, 'Genuis Loci – How Is It Retained Or Revived?', *Proceedings: Eighth Pedestrian Conference*, The City of Boulder Transportation Division, Boulder, 1987, p. 96

3 John Brinckerhoff Jackson, *Discovering the Vernacular Landscape*, Yale University Press, New Haven, 1984, p. 36

4 Michael Conroy, 'Transport Alternatives for the Energy Disadvantaged', *Social Alternatives*, vol. 1, no. 8, Department of Government, University of Queensland, Brisbane, 1980, p. 29

5 Leah Levin, *Human Rights – Questions & Answers*, The UNESCO Press, Paris, 1981, p. 11

6 Charles Birch, *On Purpose*, New South Wales University Press, Sydney, 1990, p. 8

7 Saul D Alinsky, *Rules for Radicals*, Random House, New York, 1971, p. 22

8 Michael Renner, *Rethinking the Role of the Automobile*, Worldwatch Paper 84, Worldwatch Institute, Washington D.C., 1988, p. 35

9 ibid., p. 36

10 ibid., p. 46. In the USA, each car consumes 4,000 square feet in parking spaces (including at home) which is almost three times the living area of the average family home.

11 OECD, *The Automobile and the Environment – An International Perspective*, MIT Press, Cambridge, 1978, p. 135

12 Jane Jacobs, *The Death and Life of Great American Cities*, Random House, New York, 1961, p. 341

13 Alice Tay, *Human Rights for Australia*, Human Rights Commission Monograph Series no. 1, Australian Government Publishing Service, Canberra, 1986, p. 32

14 Hugh Stretton, *Ideas for Australian Cities*, Hugh Stretton, Adelaide, 1970, p. 106

15 Bornhorst Ward Veitch Pty Ltd, *Brisbane Travel Characteristics Study Report & Data Compendium*, Bornhorst Ward Veitch, Brisbane, 1987. Table 5–7. Non-home based trips have been subtracted from the figures provided as recommended by the consultants on pages 31 and 32 of the Study Report.

16 Andrew Jakubowicz, 'What About the People?', *Symposium – Are Urban Freeways Really Necessary?* Institution of Engineers Australia, Sydney, 1973, p. 3.10

17 CART, *Route 20 News*, Nov. 28, 1987, CART, Brisbane, 1987, p. 3

18 Ian Manning, *Beyond Walking Distance – The Gains from Speed in Australian Urban Travel*, Urban Research Unit, Australian National University, Canberra, 1984, p. 6

19 Michael Replogle, 'Let Them Drive Cars', *New Internationalist*, May 1989, New Internationalist Publications, Melbourne, 1989, p. 18

20 ibid.

21 ibid.

22 Cited, Wayne Ellwood, 'Car Chaos', *New Internationalist*, May 1989 New Internationalist Publications, Melbourne, 1989, p. 6

23 Michael Renner, *Rethinking the Role of the Automobile*, Worldwatch Paper 84, Worldwatch Institute, Washington D.C., 1988, pp. 10–13

24 Stephen Plowden, *Towns Against Traffic*, Andre Deutsch, London, 1972, p. 25

25 Manning, op.cit., p. 102

26 David St. Clair, *The Motorization of American Cities*, Praeger, New York, 1986, p. 53

27 ibid., p. 69

28 Roberto Brambilla, *More Streets for People*, The Italian Art and Landscape Foundation, 1975, p. 20

29 Manning, op.cit., p. 50

30 op.cit., p. 110

31 Todd Litman, *Transportation Efficiency – An Economic Analysis*, TESC Master of Environmental Studies, Olympia, 1991.

32 Bundesminister für Raumordnung, Bauwesen und Städtbau, *Wohnstraßen der Zukunft Verkehrsberuhigung zur Verbesserung des Wohnumfeldes*, Bonn, 1979, p. 12

33 Bundesminister für Raumordnung, Bauwesen und Städtbau, *Planungsfibel zur Verkehrsberuhigung*, Bonn, 1982, p. 16

34 Jan Tanghe, Sieg Vlaeminck & Jo Berghoef, *Living Cities*, Pergamon Press, Oxford, 1984, pp. 3–6

5   Rebuilding the Eco-City together

1 Jeremiah Creedon, 'The Fantasy Machine', *New Internationalist*, May 1989, New Internationalist Publications, Melbourne, 1989, p. 10

2 Cited, Peter Hall, *Cities of Tomorrow*, Basil Blackwell, Oxford, 1988, p. 241

3 Jan Tanghe, Sieg Vlaeminck & Jo Berghoef, *Living Cities*, Pergamon Press, Oxford, 1984, p. ix

4 Cited, Ada Louise Huxtable, *Will They Ever Finish the Bruckner Boulevard: A Primer on Urbicide*, Collier Books, New York, 1972, p. 10

5 Phil Day, 'Traffic Calming', *Queensland Planner*, vol. 29, no. 1, Royal Australian Planning Institute Queensland Division, Brisbane, 1989, p. 2

6 Geoff Lacey, *What Technologies Are Appropriate?*, Pax Christi, Carlton South, Melbourne, 1989, p. 5

7 'Never on a Monday', *Sunday Sun*, Brisbane. 15/4/90

8 Hugh Stretton, *Ideas for Australian Cities*, Hugh Stretton, Adelaide, 1970, pp. 10,15

9 Cited, Peter Newman & Jeffrey Kenworthy, *Cities and Automobile Dependence – An International Source Book*, Gower Technical, Aldershot, 1989, p. 92

10 Stretton, op.cit., p. 12

11 Kenneth R. Schneider, *On the Nature of Cities*, Jossey-Bass Publication, San Francisco, 1979, p. 312

12 ibid., p. 314

13 Peter Newman & Jeffrey Kenworthy, *Cities and Automobile Dependence – An International Source Book*, Gower Technical, Aldershot, 1989, pp. 38,43. These figures have been adjusted for average speed and efficiency.

14 ibid., p. 67

15 Sim Van der Ryn & Peter Calthorpe, *Sustainable Communities*, Sierra Club Books, San Francisco, 1986, p. xiii

16 Kirby W. Lockard, 'The Pedestrian Connection: Retrofitting the Pedestrian Connections in American Cities', *Proceedings Tenth Annual International Pedestrian Conference*, The City of Boulder Transportation Division, Boulder, 1989, p. 94

17 Ian Manning, *Beyond Walking Distance – The Gains from Speed in Australian Urban Travel*, Urban Research Unit, Australian National University, Canberra, 1984, p. 126

18 ibid., p. 50

19 Schneider, op.cit., p. 80

20 Joel Woodhull, *Calmer, Not Faster: A New Direction for the Streets of L.A.*, (Draft 1.2), Southern California Rapid Transit District, Los Angeles, 1990, p. 9

21 Cited, Huxtable, op.cit., p. 10

22 Jane Jacobs, *The Death and Life of Great American Cities*, Random House, New York, 1961, pp. 368–370

23 Charles Birch, *On Purpose*, New South Wales University Press, Sydney, 1990, p. xvii

Select bibliography

Adams, John G.V. *Risk and Freedom.* Sarn Litho Printers, Gwynedd, Wales, 1988.

Alinsky, Saul D. *Rules for Radicals.* Random House, New York, 1971.

Appleyard, Donald. *Livable Streets.* University of California Press, Berkeley, 1981.

Banks, Robert. *The Tyranny of Time.* Lancer, Sydney, 1985.

Bates, John W. & Lawrence, J. Dewel. 'Transit Marketing: A Strategic Approach.' *Transportation Quarterly.* vol. 40, no. 4, October 1986, pp. 549–58.

Bendixson, Terence. *Instead of Cars.* Temple Smith, London, 1974.

Berman, Marshal. 'Among the Ruins.' *New Internationalist*, December 1987, pp. 8–9.

Birch, Charles. *On Purpose.* New South Wales University Press, Sydney, 1990.

Black, John. *Urban Transport Planning.* Croom Helm, London, 1981.

Bode, Peter M., Hamberger, Sylvia & Zängl, Wolfgang. *Alptraum Auto.* Raben Verlag, München, 1989.

Bornhorst Ward Veitch Pty. Ltd. *Brisbane Travel Characteristics Study Report & Data Compendium.* Bornhorst Ward Veitch, Brisbane, 1987.

Bowyer, D.P. & Briggs, D.C. *System Indicators to Aid Urban Road Management.* Publication AIR, pp. 342–5, Australian Road Research Board, Vermont South, 1982.

Brambilla, Roberto. *More Streets for People.* The Italian Art and Landscape Foundation, 1975.

—— *For Pedestrians Only: Planning Design and Management of Traffic Free Zones.* Witney Library of Design, New York, 1977.

Brindle, Ray. *Town Planning and Road Safety.* Publication CR33, Office of Road Safety, Canberra, 1984.

—— 'Never Mind the Width – Feel the Quality!' *Australian Planner* vol. 27, no. 3, September 1989, pp. 19–28.

—— *Design of the Local Distributor: Special Report.* Director General of Transport, South Australia, undated.

Bruton, M.J. 'The "Traffic in Towns" Philosophy: Current Relevance.' *Built Environment* vol. 9, no. 2, pp. 99–101.

Bundesminister für Raumordnung, Bauwesen und Städtbau. *Wohnstraßen der Zukunft Verkehrsberuhigung zur Verbesserung des Wohnumfeldes.* Bonn, 1979.

—— *Planungsfibel zur Verkehrsberuhigung.* Bonn, 1982.

CART. *Route 20 News.* November 28, 1987.

Cartwright, T. 'Planning and Chaos Theory.' *Journal of the American Planning Association*, vol. 57, no 1, Winter 1991, pp. 44–56.

Conroy, Michael. 'Transport Alternatives for the Energy Disadvantaged.' *Social Alternatives.* vol. 1, no 8, pp. 29–33.

Crauston, Maurice. *What Are Human Rights.* Bodley Head, London, 1973.

Creedon, Jeremiah. 'The Fantasy Machine.' *New Internationalist.* May 1989, pp. 9–10.

Cutler, Laurence Stephan & Stephens-Cutler, Sherrie. 'Establishing a Dialog for Recycling Cities.' *Ekistics*, 256 March 1977, pp. 165–71.

Daes, Erica-Irene A. *The Individuals Duties to the Community and the Limitations on Human Rights and the Freedoms Under Article 29 of the Universal Declaration of Human Rights.* United Nations, New York, 1983.

Daniels, P.W. & Warnes, A.M. *Movement in Cities: Spacial Perspectives On Urban Transport and Travel.* Methuen, London, 1983.

Danish Road Directorate. *Consequence Evaluation of Environmentally Adapted Through Roads in Vinderup*, Road Data Laboratory Report 52. Copenhagen, 1987.

—— *Consequence Evaluation of Environmentally Adapted Through Roads in Skærbæk*, Road Data Laboratory Report 63. Copenhagen, 1988.

Davidson, K.B. 'Use of Accessibility in Metropolitan Strategic Planning.' *Transport Planning and Evaluation.* vol. 9. Australian Road Research Board, Vermont South, 1978, 1401 1416.

Deen, Thomas B. & Goodwin, Stephen R. 'Safety Benefits of the 55 MPH Speed Limit.' *Transportation Quarterly.* vol. 39, no. 3, July 1985, pp. 321–43.

Der Minister für Stadtentwicklung, Wohnen und Verkehr des Landes Nordrhein-Westfalen. *Parke Nicht Auf Unseren Wegen*. Report, 5–88.

—— *Sicherer Verkehr, Ortsgerechte Straßen*. Report, 3–89.

—— *Radverkehr-wegweisend in die Zukunft*. Report, 5–89.

Elliott, Barry. *Children and Road Accidents: An Analysis of the Problems and Some Suggested Solutions*. Report no. CR36, Federal Office of Road Safety, Canberra, 1985.

Ellul, Jacques. *The Technological Society*. Vintage Books, New York, 1964.

Ellwood, Wayne. 'Car Chaos.' *New Internationalist* May 1989, pp. 4–7.

Engwicht, David (ed). *Traffic Calming – The Solution to Route 20 and a New Vision for Brisbane*. CART, Brisbane, 1989.

—— 'Access Efficiency Enhancement – More Saleable Than "Demand Management" & Providing a New Suite of System-wide Indicators.' *1991 International Transport Conference – Preprints of Papers*. Institute of Engineers, Australia National Conference Publication no. 91/4, Canberra, 1991, pp. 1–7.

Fox, Matthew. *Original Blessing*. Bear and Company, Santa Fe, New Mexico, 1986.

Gakenheimer, Ralph (ed). *The Automobile and the Environment: An International Perspective*. MIT Press, Cambridge, 1978.

Gleick, James. *Chaos – Making a New Science*. Sphere Books, London, 1990.

Gray, D.A. (ed). *Acoustics and Society: Proceedings of the 1981 Annual Conference of the Australian Acoustical Society*.

Great Britain Ministry of Transport. *Better Use of Town Roads: The Report of a Study of the Means of Restraint of Traffic on Urban Roads*. Her Majesty's Stationary Office, London, 1967.

Hajdu, J.G. 'Pedestrian Malls in West Germany: Perceptions of Their Role and Stages in Their Development.' *APA Journal* Summer 1988, pp. 325–35.

Hall, Peter. *Great Planning Disasters*. California Series in Urban Development vol. 1. University of California Press, 1982.

—— *Cities of Tomorrow*. Basil Blackwell, Oxford, 1988.

Hall, Peter & Hass-Klau, Carman. *Can Rail Save the City?* Gower, Brookfield, VT, 1985.

Hart, Gordon E., Elliot, Claudi & Lamare, Judith. *Heading the Wrong Way: Redirecting California's Transportation Policies.* Sierra Club Green State of the State Report 1990, Sacremento.

Hass-Klau, Carmen. *The Theory and Practice of Traffic Calming: Can Britain Learn From the German Experience?* Ress Jeffrey's Road Fund Transport and Society Discussion Paper 10, Oxford, 1990.

—— *An Illustrated Guide to Traffic Calming.* Friends of the Earth, London, 1990.

—— (ed). 'New Ways of Managing Traffic.' *Built Environment.* vol. 12, no. 1/2, pp. 4–97.

Hillman, Mayer. 'The Wrong Turning: Twenty Years on from Buchanan.' *Built Environment.* vol. 9, no. 2, pp. 104–11.

Huxtable, Ada Louise. *Will They Ever Finish the Bruckner Boulevard: A Primer on Urbicide.* Collier Books, New York, 1972.

Illich, Ivan. *Energy and Equity.* Marion Boyars, London, 1979.

Institution of Engineers Australia. *Symposium – Are Urban Freeways Really Necessary?* Institution of Engineers Australia, Sydney, 1973.

Jackson, John Brinckerhoff. *Discovering the Vernacular Landscape.* Yale University Press, New Haven, 1984.

Jacobs, Jane. *The Death and Life of Great American Cities.* Random House, New York, 1961.

Karlqvist, Anders et al (eds). *Spatial Interaction Theory and Planning Models.* North-Holland Publishing Company, Amsterdam, 1978.

Kellermann, Bill. 'Discerning the Angel of Detroit.' *Sojourners,* October 1989, vol. 18, no 9, pp. 16–21. Washington DC, 1989.

King, Graham A.D. '"No Particular Place": A Meditation on Mobility.' *The Planner TCPSS Proceedings 23 February, 1990,* pp. 43–6.

King, Joe J.R. 'Adequacy of Transportation in Minority Communities for Handicapped, Low Income and Elderly Groups.' *Transportation Quarterly.* vol. 41, no. 2, April 1989, pp. 247–61.

King, R.J. 'Some Problems in Assessing the Social Effects of Transport Related Plans.' *Australian Road Research.* vol. 13, no.. 4, December 1983, pp. 271–84.

Kirby, D.S. *Report by D.S. Kirby, B.A., LL.B, of the Commission of Inquiry Into the Kyeemagh–Chullora Road*. D. West Government Printer, New South Wales, 1981.

Koenig, J.G. 'Indicators of Urban Accessibility: Theory and Application.' *Transportation 9.* vol. 9, 1980, pp. 145–72.

Lacey, Geoff. *South Australian Energy Future: The Sustainable Option*. Friends of the Earth, Adelaide, 1986.

—— *What Technologies Are Appropriate?* Pax Christi. Carlton South, Melbourne, 1989.

Lacoute, P. *The Environment of Human Settlement: Human Well-being in Cities*. Pergamon, Oxford, 1976.

Levin, Leah. *Human Rights – Questions & Answers*. The UNESCO Press, Paris, 1981.

Levinson, Herbert S. 'Streets For People and Transit.' *Transportation Quarterly.* vol. 40, no. 4, October 1986, pp. 503–20.

Lin, Ben C. 'Transportation Improvement Districts.' *Urban Land.* June 1987, pp. 32–3.

Litman, Todd. *Transportation Efficiency – An Economic Analysis*. TESC Master of Environmental Studies, Olympia, 1991.

Lowe, Marcia D. *The Bicycle: Vehicle for a Small Planet*. Worldwatch Paper 90, Worldwatch Institute, Washington, DC, 1989.

—— *Alternatives to the Automobile: Transport for Livable Cities*. Worldwatch Paper 98, Worldwatch Institute, Washington, DC, 1990.

McNulty, Robert et al. *Return of the Livable City in America*. Partners for Livable Places, Acropolis Books, Washington, DC, 1986.

'Make Them Pay'. *The Economist.* February 18, 1989, pp. 11–22.

Manning, Ian. *Beyond Walking Distance – The Gains from Speed in Australian Urban Travel*. Urban Research Unit, Australian National University, Canberra, 1984.

Marsh, Peter & Collett, Peter. 'Driving Passion.' *Psychology Today.* June 1987, pp. 16–24.

Moriarty, Patrick & Beed, Clive. 'Reducing Vehicular Travel Need Through Increasing Travel Efficiency.' *Urban Policy and Research*, vol. 7, no. 4, Oxford University Press, South Melbourne, 1989, pp. 157–63.

Morris, J.M., Dumble, P.L. & Wigan, M.R. *Accessibility Indicators For Transport Planning*. Publication ARR 102, Australian Road Research Board, Vermont South, 1979.

Mumford, Lewis. *The City in History*. Penguin, Harmondsworth, 1966.

—— *The Myth of the Machine*. Harcourt, Brace & World, New York. 1967.

Nelson, P.M. (ed). *Transportation Noise Reference Book*. Butterworths, London, 1987.

Newman, Peter. 'An Ecological Model for City Structure and Development.' *Ekistics* 239, October 1975, pp. 258–65.

—— *Social Organization for Ecological Sustainability: Toward a More Sustainable Settlement Pattern*. Environmental Science, Murdoch University, undated.

Newman, Peter & Kenworthy, Jeffrey. *Cities and Automobile Dependence – An International Source Book*. Gower Technical, Aldershot, 1989.

OECD. *The Automobile and the Environment – An International Perspective*. MIT Press, Cambridge, 1978.

Oram, Richard L. 'Making Transit Passes Viable in the 1980s.' *Transportation Quarterly*. vol. 37, no. 2, April 1983, pp. 289–96.

Orski, Kenneth C. 'Transportation Management Associations: Battling Suburban Traffic Congestion.' *Urban Land*. December 1986, pp. 2–5.

—— '"Managing" Suburban Traffic Congestion: A Strategy for Suburban Mobility.' *Transportation Quarterly*. vol. 41, no. 4, October 1987, pp. 457–76.

Owen, Wilfred. *The Accessible City*. The Brookings Institution, Washington, DC, 1972.

Parliamentary Commissioner for the Environment. Audit of the 'Future State of the Highway Number One Route'. *Environmental Impact Report*. Wellington, 1990.

Plowden, Stephen. *Towns Against Traffic*. Andre Deutsch, London, 1972.

—— *Taming Traffic*. Andre Deutsch, London, 1980.

—— *Changing the Rules*. Publication 642, Policy Studies Insititute, London, 1985.

Plowden, Stephen & Hillman, Mayer. *Danger on the Road: the Needless Scourge*. Publication 627, Policy Studies Institute, London, 1984.

Porter, Douglas R. 'The Future Doesn't Work.' *TR News.* November–December 1987, pp. 14–5.

Pressman, N. (ed). *International Experiences in Creating Livable Cities.* Faculty of Environmental Studies, University of Waterloo, Canada, 1981.

Pucher, John. 'A Comparison Analysis of Policies and Travel Behaviour in the Soviet Union, Eastern and Western Europe, and North America.' *Transportation Quarterly.* vol. 44, no. 3, July 1990, pp. 441–65.

Railway Industry Council. *Rail Into the 21st Century: A Railway Industry Discussion Paper.* Australian Government Publishing Service, Canberra, 1990.

—— *Conclusions and Recommendations.* Canberra, 1990.

Renner, Michael. *Rethinking the Role of the Automobile.* Worldwatch Paper 84, Worldwatch Institute, Washington D.C., 1988.

Replogle, Michael. 'Let Them Drive Cars.' *The New Internationalist,* May 1989, pp. 18–9.

Roberts, John. *Pedestrian Precincts in Britain.* TEST, London, 1981.

—— 'Where's Downtown?' *Town and Country Planning.* May 1988, pp. 138–41.

Roberts, John et al. *The Big Choke.* TEST and London Weekend Television, London, 1989.

Rudofsky, Bernard. *Streets for People – A Primer for Americans.* Doubleday & Company, New York, 1969.

Rybczynski, Witold. 'Living Smaller.' *The Alantic Monthly.* February 1991, pp. 64–78.

Schaeffer, K.H. & Sclar, Elliott. *Access for All: Transportation and Urban Growth.* Penguin Books, Harmondsworth, 1975.

Schneider, Kenneth R. *On the Nature of Cities.* Jossey-Bass Publication, San Francisco, 1979.

Schonfeld, Paul M. & Chadda, Himmat S. 'An Assesment of Urban Travel Reduction Options.' *Transportation Quarterly.* vol. 39, no. 3, July 1985, pp. 391–406.

Simpson, Rod. 'Life, Liberty and the Pursuit of Clean Air.' *Habitat.* vol. 16, no. 2, April 1988, pp. 11–4.

Song, Linda. 'A Comparison of Travel in Sydney and Beijing.' *Australian Road Research.* vol. 19, no. 3, September 1989.

Spearritt, Peter. *Make Way for the Car: Transport in the Metro Plans.* Urban Research Unit, Australian National University, Canberra, 1989.

Stapleton, Christopher. *Planning and Road Design for New Residential Subdivisions: Guidelines.* Director General of Transport, South Australia, undated.

—— *Planning and Road Design for New Residential Sub divisions: Supplement to Guidelines.* Director General of Transport, South Australia, undated.

Starkie, D.N.M. *Transportation Planning, Policy and Analysis.* Pergamon Press, Oxford, 1976.

St. Clair, David. *The Motorization of American Cities.* Praeger, New York, 1986.

Stretton, Hugh. *Ideas for Australian Cities.* Hugh Stretton, Adelaide, 1970.

Tay, Alice. *Human Rights for Australia.* Human Rights Commission Monograph Series no. 1, Australian Government Publishing Service, Canberra, 1986.

Tanghe, J., Vlaeminck, S. & Berghoef, J. *Living Cities.* Pergamon Press, Oxford, 1984.

TEST. *Quality Streets.* TEST, London, 1988.

Thomson, J. Michael. *Great Cities and Their Traffic.* Penguin, Harmondsworth, 1978.

Tobias, Andrew. 'Fill 'Er Up With No-Fault Please.' *Time Magazine.* February 27, 1989, pp. 52–3.

Tolley, Rodney (ed). *The Greening of Urban Transport.* Belhaven Press, London, 1990.

'A Town That Cares For Kids.' *Parents and Children.* July, 1989, pp. 24–5.

'Traffic Jams: The City, the Commuter and the Car.' *The Economist.* February 18, 1989, pp. 11–22.

Transportation Division, City of Boulder. *Proceedings: The Third Annual Pedestrian Conference.* City of Boulder, Colorado, 1982.

—— *Proceedings: The Fourth Annual Pedestrian Conference.* City of Boulder, Colorado, 1983.

—— *Proceedings: The Fifth Annual Pedestrian Conference.* City of Boulder, Colorado, 1984.

—— *Proceedings: The Sixth Annual Pedestrian Conference*. City of Boulder, Colorado, 1985.

—— *Proceedings: The Seventh Annual Pedestrian Conference*. City of Boulder, Colorado, 1986.

—— *Proceedings: The Eighth Annual Pedestrian Conference*. City of Boulder, Colorado, 1987.

—— *Proceedings: The Ninth Annual International Pedestrian Conference*. City of Boulder, Colorado, 1988.

—— *Proceedings: The Tenth Annual International Pedestrian Conference*. City of Boulder, Colorado, 1989.

University of New South Wales. *Transporting People*. Occasional Papers no. 4, 1979.

Van der Ryn, Sim & Calthorpe, Peter. *Sustainable Communities*. Sierra Club Books, San Francisco, 1986.

Vickery, Peter. 'Traffic Is A Health Hazard.' *Legal Service Bulletin*. December 1978, pp. 237–41.

Ward, Colin. 'Community Architecture: What A Time It Took For the Penny to Drop!' *Built Environment*. vol. 13 no. 1, pp. 7–13.

Wardroper, John. *Juggernaut*. Temple Smith, London, 1981.

Webster, F.V. et al. *Changing Patterns of Urban Travel*. Transport and Road Research Laboratory, United Kingdom, 1985.

Weigelt, Horst R., Götz, Rainer E. & Weiss, Helmut H. *City Traffic: A Systems Digest*. Trans. Gunther F Wengatz. Van Nostrand Reinfold, New York, 1977.

White, Deborah et al. *Seeds for Change*. Conservation Council of Victoria and Patchwork Press, Melbourne, 1978.

Ying, Li Jia. 'Management of Bicycling in Urban Areas.' *Transportation Quarterly*. vol. 41, no. 4, October 1987, pp. 619–29.

Index